THE ONEONTA ROUNDHOUSE

Jim Loudon

Second Edition

SQUARE CIRCLE PRESS
VOORHEESVILLE, NEW YORK

The Oneonta Roundhouse

Published by
Square Circle Press LLC
137 Ketcham Road
Voorheesville, NY 12186
www.squarecirclepress.com

Copyright © 1993, 2010 by Jim Loudon.
All rights reserved. No part of this publication may be reproduced or transmitted in any form, or by any means, electronic or mechanical, without permission in writing from the publisher, except by a reviewer who wishes to quote brief passages for inclusion in a magazine, newspaper or broadcast.

Second edition, 2010.
Printed and bound in the United States of America on acid-free, durable paper.

ISBN 13: 978-0-9789066-9-9
ISBN 10: 0-9789066-8-9
Library of Congress Control Number: 2010942120

Cover photo: The Oneonta Roundhouse, circa 1945.

Author's Acknowledgments

It is difficult to thank all the people who helped make the first, and now second edition of this book possible, as there have been so many individuals who have assisted in so many ways. Special thanks goes to Tim Truscott of the Mohawk & Hudson Chapter, NRHS for supplying us with rare documentation on the roundhouse construction and for introducing us to the New York State Library Special Collection. Special thanks also goes to the staff members at Huntington Library in Oneonta, The New York State Historical Association Library in Cooperstown and the New York State Archives in Albany. A very special thank you goes to Fran Green, Huntington Library Historian for helping to tie together the many loose ends in the story. Also, special thanks to Mrs. Wilmer Bresee of Oneonta for allowing us to copy several photographs from her private collection and to Ray Baker, great-grandson of Harvey Baker, for providing us with a portrait of his famous ancestor. And last, but not least, special thanks to LRHS President Bruce Hodges and his mom Millie for the many long hours they spent copying documents at the National Records Center in Washington, D.C.

CONTENTS

PREFACE TO THE SECOND EDITION..........5

INTRODUCTION..........7

1: PREDECESSORS..........9

2: THE NEW ROUNDHOUSE..........19

3: IMPROVEMENTS..........35

4: THE CHALLENGERS..........59

5: THE COAL POCKET FIRE..........71

6: THE END OF AN ERA..........79

EPILOGUE..........85

SOURCES..........98

PREFACE TO THE SECOND EDITION

It doesn't seem possible that T*he Oneonta Roundhouse* is over ten years old now, and is still in great demand. The adventure began in late 1992 when I decided to tackle my first book, after writing several articles on local railroad history. After months of research, trips to the New York State Library and the ordeal of learning how to navigate thru the Pagemaker program and assemble the various pieces into a coherent book, the finished product arrived in November 1993. One of the last projects in the process was shooting several rolls of film in and around the remaining seventeen stalls of what was once the largest roundhouse in the world. Little did I know, I was working against the clock—within one month what was left of this monumental structure would be brought to the ground, leaving nothing behind but a smokestack and a pile of bricks. From this date the only tangible documentation of the great building is my book and an outstanding documentary, "All the Live Long Day," produced by Gerard Meola of New York City.

The real challenge came once the books were in hand—would all the work be worthwhile? Would anyone actually buy the book? Since I made the decision to self-publish the financial risk was mine alone and I prayed for the best. The initial printing was 1,000 copies, and I was amazed at how quickly they sold. Over the next few years I would go through two more printings of 1,000 copies. Unfortunately, after the third printing I found out that it would be impossible to engage a fourth printing as the printer had destroyed the plates when the company reorganized. Because of this, the book went out-of-print for nearly ten years unitil I was fortunate enough to discover Square Circle Press, which brought the book back to life. The process was arduous, as we had to basically recreate the entire book in digital format, but the effort was worth it, the new book being even better quality than the original. With a short run of 250 more copies being exhausted, we decided it was time to update to a second edition, which has a new cover, a table of contents, and a few revisions to the text (mainly clean-up). My hope is that the second edition will continue to be as successful and enduring as the first.

Jim Loudon
Oneonta, New York

Harvey Baker

INTRODUCTION

Prior to 1865, the area now occupied by the Delaware and Hudson's Oneonta Shops was part of a vast swamp, several miles long and nearly a mile wide in some places. Were it not for the tireless efforts of one man, Harvey Baker, this land would never have been developed and the shop complex that transformed Oneonta into a major rail center would have been located elsewhere.

Harvey Baker was a prosperous and farsighted Oneonta businessman, operating a large mill complex which included a foundry and machine shop. Mr. Baker also acquired sizable land holdings in and around Oneonta, including much of what would eventually become the commercial hub of the village.

Harvey Baker was convinced early on that it was critical for Oneonta's future to be connected by rail to the outside world and he expended tremendous personal energy and capital to ensure the realization of his vision. Assuming the position of director once the Albany and Susquehanna had been chartered, he was also one of the principal stockholders. Once construction had begun, he was appointed general agent for the company, securing right-of-way and building materials, in addition to personally supervising erection of trestles along the line and overseeing completion of the road from Cobleskill to Oneonta.

Harvey Baker's greatest contribution, however, was in securing the location of the Albany and Susquehanna shop facilities. As the line was progressing south from Cobleskill, there was strong competition between Oneonta and Colliersville for this honor, both villages being desirous of the prosperity that would accompany the locomotive repair shops. Jared Goodyear, although a fellow A. & S. director and business associate of Harvey Baker, still did his best to convince the company to locate in Colliersville, named in honor of his father-in-law, Peter Collier. Jared even agreed to donate the land for the facility, and the Company eagerly accepted his generous offer.

Harvey Baker, however, was not willing to relinquish Oneonta's future without a fight. He and A. & S. director Eliakim Ford convinced Jared Goodyear to provide the Company with an option on the properties he owned in the village, if they were found to be suitable for a shop complex. Through this brilliant bit of maneuvering, Mr. Baker and Mr. Ford opened the door for the Albany and Susquehanna to locate their shops in Oneonta, forever ending Colliersville's dream of becoming a prosperous railroad town.

The location finally agreed upon was actually west of the Goodyear property and, once it had been obtained, work was begun immediately draining and filling the swamp, with the first roundhouse being constructed in the fall of 1870. The line and the shops grew steadily, adding another roundhouse and several repair buildings over the years. Finally the facility outgrew itself and in 1906 Oneonta witnessed the construction of the largest roundhouse the world had ever known.

CHAPTER ONE

PREDECESSORS

From the time the Albany and Susquehanna Railroad reached Oneonta in 1865, until 1868, the village possessed no facilities to protect the Company's locomotives from the elements, so motive power was stored at other points on the line. The first engine house to be located in Oneonta was a crude structure that had been moved up from Harpursville in the spring of 1868. This building was about 100 feet long and had been erected by Harvey Baker, who was the primary contractor for the Company at the time. This building was intended to serve as a temporary shelter for the engines until a permanent facility could be constructed.

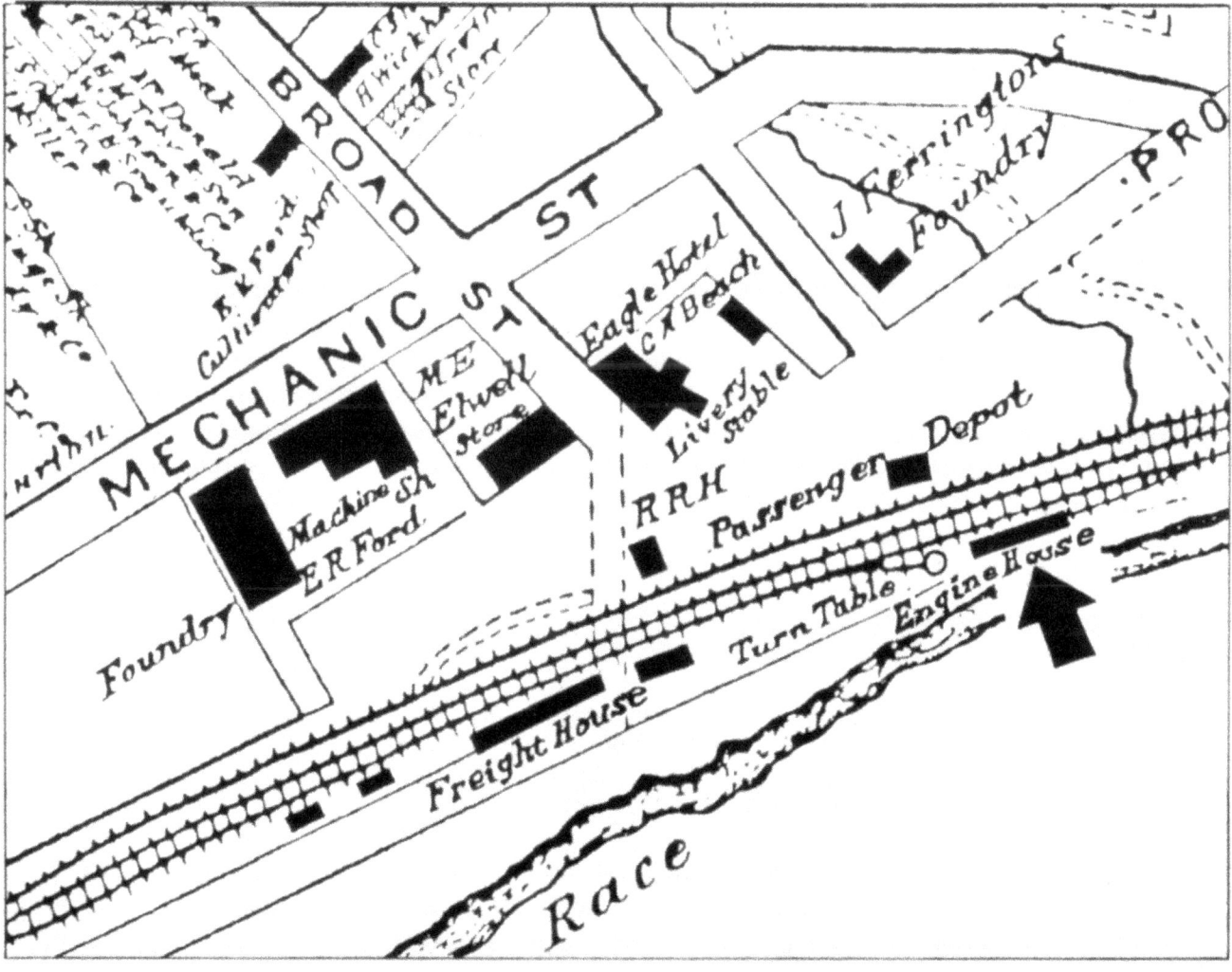

Albany & Susquehanna Yard Complex at Oneonta, circa 1868. At this time the entire facility was located adjacent to the passenger depot, with no development below the Main Street crossing. The arrow indicates the first engine house, which was brought up from Harpursville by Harvey Baker. No photographs of this building are known to exist. (Atlas of Otsego County, 1868)

During this period there was intense competition between Oneonta and Colliersville to be the village selected as the main shop facility for the Albany and Susquehanna. Early on during construction, the road had made an agreement with Jared Goodyear to locate the shops in Colliers in exchange for his donation of all the required property. This agreement did not set well with the businessmen of Oneonta, Harvey Baker in particular. Mr. Baker and his business associate Eliakim Ford expended a great deal of effort attempting to sway Jared Goodyear away from his agreement with the A. & S. One very effective point of persuasion was the fact that Jared possessed extensive land holdings in Oneonta, mostly adjacent to the rail line and ideally situated for development into a shop complex.

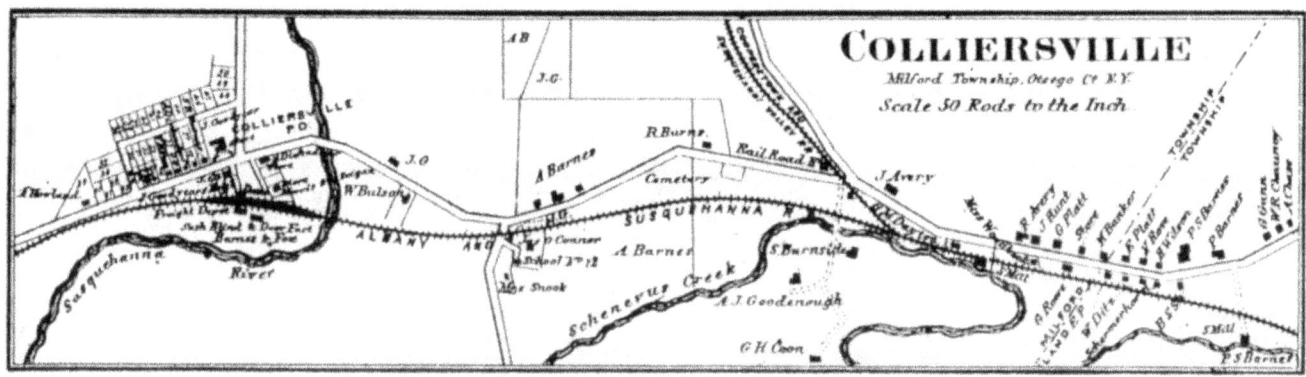

The village of Colliersville, as it appeared in 1868. If Jared Goodyear had been successful convincing the Albany & Susquehanna to locate their shops here, this tiny hamlet might have rivaled Oneonta in growth and prosperity. (Note: At this early date, Cooperstown Junction had not yet acquired its title, as the depot was not constructed until the following year.) (Atlas of Otsego County, 1868)

The arguments were obviously convincing, as Harvey Baker obtained a contract from Mr. Goodyear on November 4, 1869, in which the latter agreed to sell whatever lands he owned that would be found suitable for construction of an engine or round house. All evidence indicates that Harvey Baker personally did not consider the Goodyear lands to be the best location for the shops, but by obtaining the option from Jared, he effectively cleared the way for Oneonta to be considered as a potential site, confident that Company officials would find a tract in the village that would meet their requirements. Two days later Colonel Coryel, assistant to A. & S. Chief Engineer C. W. Wentz, visited Oneonta to inspect the Goodyear property and decide on the best potential site for the shops. On this first visit, Mr. Coryel did not find a location on the property that he felt was appropriate for the Company's needs so the project was temporarily delayed.

In the meantime, while the two villages had been battling over the location of the shops, the ownership of the road itself had been in dispute. The last six months of 1869 had witnessed the famous "Railroad War" when Jim Fisk and Jay Gould attempted to pirate the Albany and Susquehanna away from its rightful owners. After months of judicial maneuvering, the war culminated in an all-out melee at Tunnel, New York on August 10. The State Militia was called in and the line was run by the Governor until it was leased to the Delaware and Hudson Canal Company on February 5, 1870.

By the summer of 1870, the construction of an engine house in Oneonta became a matter of urgency as the old structure that had been transplanted from Harpursville was inadequate for the needs of the growing Company. In early September, a delegation from the main office traveled to Oneonta, once again in search of an ideal shop location. The officials were met in Oneonta by Mr. Baker and Mr. Ford, both of whom were mutually committed to keeping the shop facility as close to the depot and business section of the village as possible. The delegation first explored the locale east of Oneonta, traveling as far as the Couse farm near the village limits but found no promising sites. Harvey Baker then suggested looking at the property just west of the depot on the Watkins farm which, he had already decided, would be the most advantageous location for the facility.

The Albany delegation was in total agreement with Mr. Baker on the suitability of this site and it was agreed that the D. & H. would locate their shops on this property if a parcel of sufficient size could be obtained. A public meeting was held and money was soon raised to purchase 20 acres of land adjacent to the Main Street bluff. Once the agreement had been made matters moved swiftly. On September 16, Chief Engineer Wentz was in Oneonta surveying the tract for roundhouse and shop positions and on the 23rd Harvey Baker paid the balance on the purchase price and took possession of the deeds. By the 24th, bids were received for erection of the first half of the south roundhouse, the contract being awarded to a Mr. Bridgeford of Albany. The specifications called for a building of 11 stalls, each one having a length of 65 feet and a width of 13 feet at the doors, tapering to 25 feet, 8 inches at the wall. The turntable was to be a balanced unit, 60 feet long. The stone, lime and cement used in construction came from Mr. Baker's plant in Howe's Cave while all the bricks for the project were fired at the Richard's plant in Oneonta's west end.

This map of Oneonta, drawn in 1868 shows: 1.) The property of Jared Goodyear that was rejected as a potential shop site; 2.) the Watkins property that was promoted by Harvey Baker and accepted by the Albany & Susquehanna as a shop facility location; 3.) The Scrambling property that was purchased by the Company in 1881 for a new roundhouse site, but was never developed. (Atlas of Otsego County, 1868)

By November of 1870, much of the construction work on the roundhouse had been completed and laborers were grading roadbed from the building site to the D. & H. main. Severe weather brought the work to a halt in December and, when it was resumed in January, a new contractor had taken over the project, John M. Farrell of Oneonta. The building was completed that month and on January 18 it was inspected and accepted by Company officials. The only work remaining was the installation of a water tank to enable locomotives to take on water while standing in their stalls. On August 3 of the same year, John Farrell and Jay McDonald were contracted to enlarge the south roundhouse, doubling its size to 22 stalls.

In spite of the enthusiasm generated by the construction of the shop facilities, some individuals in the village expressed dissatisfaction with their location. One Oneonta newspaper, "Home and Abroad," complained that the heavy locomotive traffic interfered with the main thoroughfare from Delaware county into Oneonta. In addition to the congestion at the Main Street crossing, the paper contended that the numerous engines posed a hazard to the workers enroute to the nearby mills and the argument was made that this dangerous situation could have been avoided if the shops had been built closer to the depot. Fortunately for the village, that area had been dismissed as it would not have allowed the space required by the rapidly expanding repair facility. The congestion at Main Street remained a problem, however, until a viaduct was constructed at the site in 1904.

The original Oneonta Roundhouses, circa 1881. The south roundhouse is on the left, partially obscured by locomotive steam. The north roundhouse, still under construction, is on the right. Note the early ball signal in front of the track shanty. (Bruce Mack)

The village and the railroad grew rapidly together and by 1872 the D. & H. was once again outgrowing its facilities. In April of that year, Mr. Fonda and Mr. Blackall of the Compan's main office were in Oneonta establishing locations for the long awaited shop complex. Before returning to Albany, the officials announced the immediate commencement of construction on an engine repair shop, which would be followed by a foundry and a second roundhouse. The roundhouse enlargement project, which had been temporarily suspended while the shop buildings were being laid out, was not resumed until April of 1876. The second half of the south roundhouse, comprised of 11 stalls, was completed and put into use in May of 1876.

Five years after the south roundhouse had been enlarged, the Delaware and Hudson was again experiencing a shortage of locomotive service facilities at the Oneonta terminal. At this point the Company decided it would be more practical to construct one large roundhouse than to build any more small ones. This decision led to the purchase of 50 acres of the Scrambling property off River Street, at $200.00 per acre, in June of 1881. The D. & H. management announced plans to begin construction on a new roundhouse of substantial capacity at this site in the near future but later decided to contain their operations on the north side of the right-of-way and the property was eventually sold for residential development.

After the Scrambling property had been abandoned, the Company began construction on a second engine house which would contain 15 stalls to be located within the existing shop complex, a short distance from the original roundhouse. The stalls in this building would again be 65 feet long but the turntable length was increased to 75 feet. The building was contracted by James Ackroyd of Albany and the excavation was done in August of 1881, with the brickwork being completed the following month. Work continued into the winter and the north roundhouse was inspected by and officially opened for use on January 7, 1882.

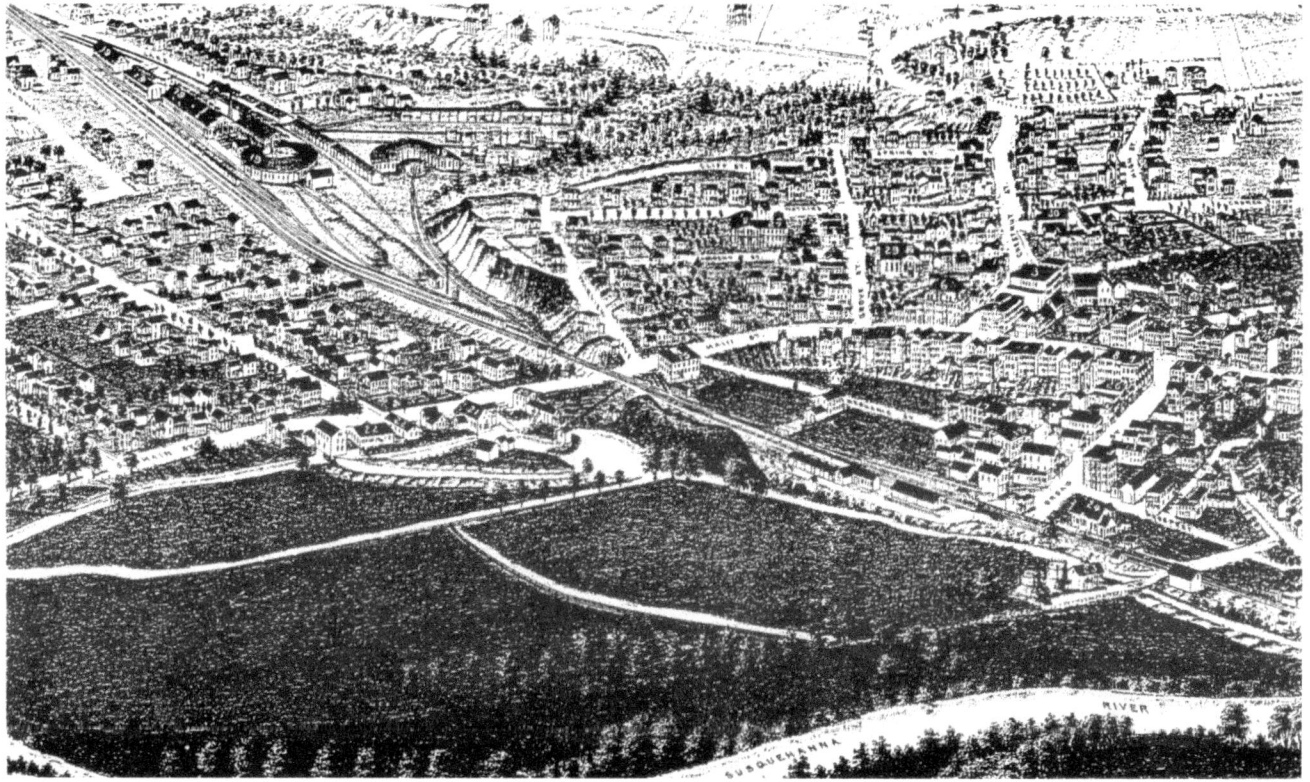

By 1884 the Albany & Susquehanna's facility at Oneonta had grown dramatically, expanding onto the former Watkins property west of Main Street. The complex included several repair shops, a foundry and two roundhouses. (Burleigh's Illustrated Map of Oneonta, 1884)

On February 23, 1882, a D. & H. delegation including General Manager Coe F. Young, Superintendent C. D. Hammond and Master Mechanic R.C. Blackall inspected the new building and outlined further expansion plans for the Oneonta facility. One segment of the expansion called for the enlargement of the second roundhouse to the same size as the older building but work on this project was never initiated and Oneonta would not see a major engine terminal developed until after the turn of the century.

The original Oneonta Roundhouses as they appeared about 1900. The building on the left is the south roundhouse, the first half of which was begun in the fall of 1870 and completed in January of 1871. Its size was doubled to 22 stalls in May of 1876. The building on the right, the north roundhouse, contained 15 stalls and was started in August of 1881 and completed in January of 1882. The first coal pocket can be seen in the left hand photo, but the piles of cord wood indicate that the Company was still in the process of converting from wood to coal burning locomotives. Note the congestion in these photos as compared to the earlier view from 1882. (Mrs. Wilmer Bresee)

After the new roundhouse was opened in 1906, the Company initially announced plans to dismantle both of the old roundhouses. However, the growing traffic on the line made it necessary to retain most of the original structures for use as supplemental repair facilities for locomotives and tenders. The north roundhouse, which became building number 20, was left intact and an 11 foot canopy was constructed over the doors of stalls 3 through 14. This allowed for servicing of the longer locomotives when necessary. The south roundhouse, which became building number 4, had 12 of it s 22 stalls removed. An addition was later attached to the east end of the building which included a storeroom, sheet metal shop and office. According to some old timers, one of these buildings was used as a recreational facility in later years and was known as "The Smoker." Both buildings were finally torn down in 1927, when the D. & H. completely reorganized its yard complex.

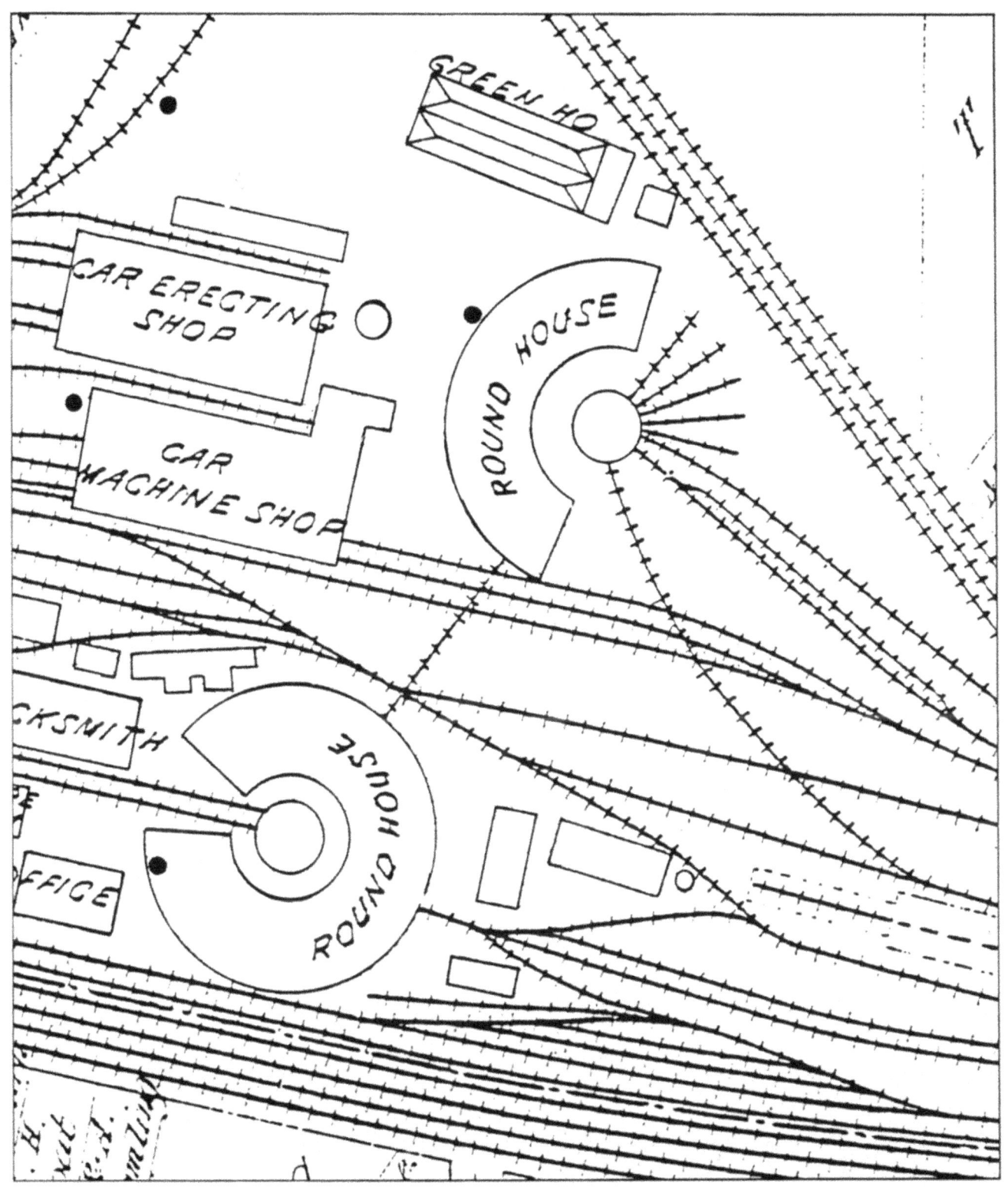

Oneonta's first roundhouses as they appeared in 1903. The north roundhouse is at the top, and the south roundhouse is at the bottom. (New Century Atlas of Otsego County, 1903)

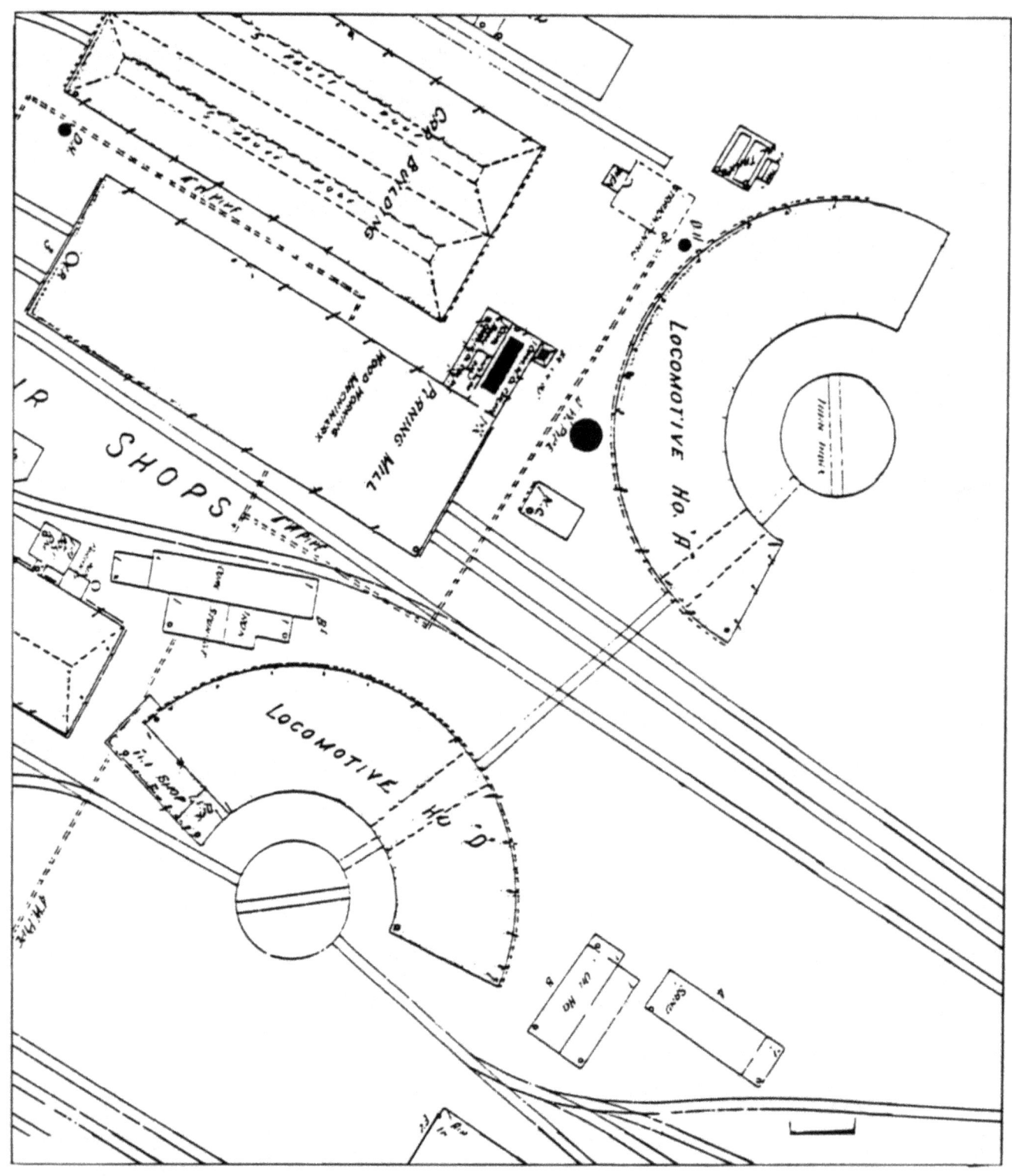

The original Oneonta Roundhouses in 1910. At this time the north roundhouse was still intact, but 12 stalls have been removed from the south roundhouse. Note the new designation of Locomotive House "A" and Locomotive House "B" respectively. (Sanborn Insurance Map Atlas of Oneonta, 1910)

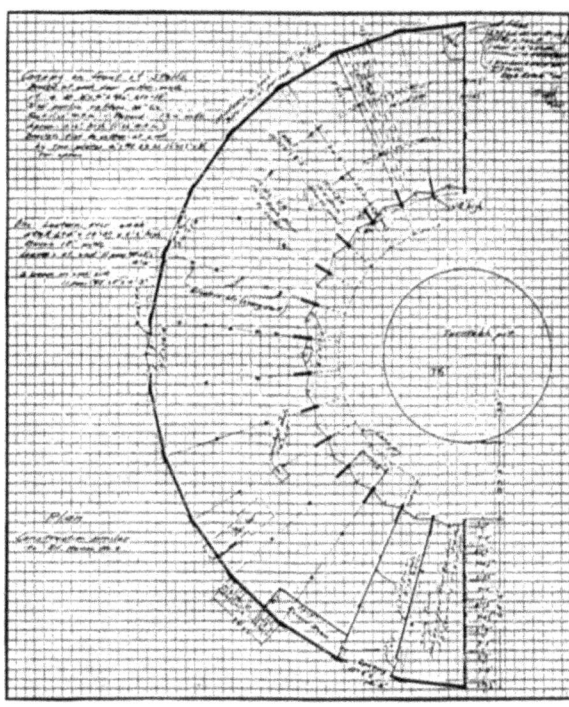

Plan of building number 20, the former north roundhouse, as it appeared in 1918. (National Records Center, Washington, D.C.)

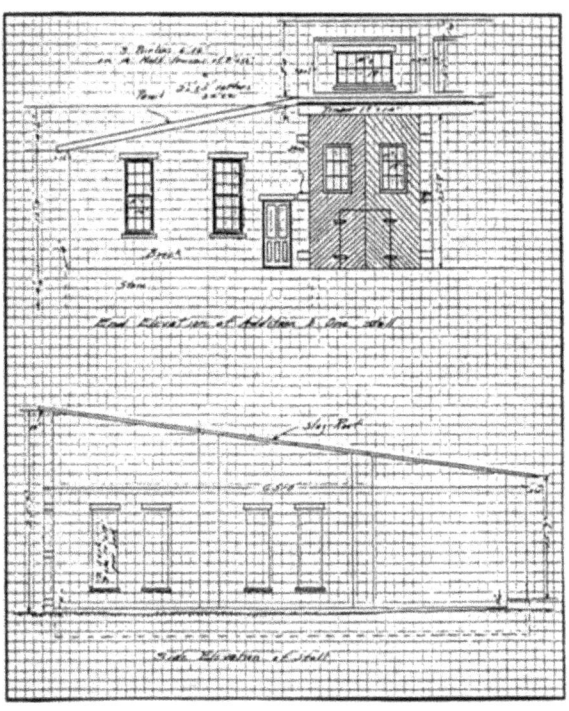

Elevation drawings of building number 4 showing sheet metal shop and typical stall. (National Records Center, Washington, D.C.)

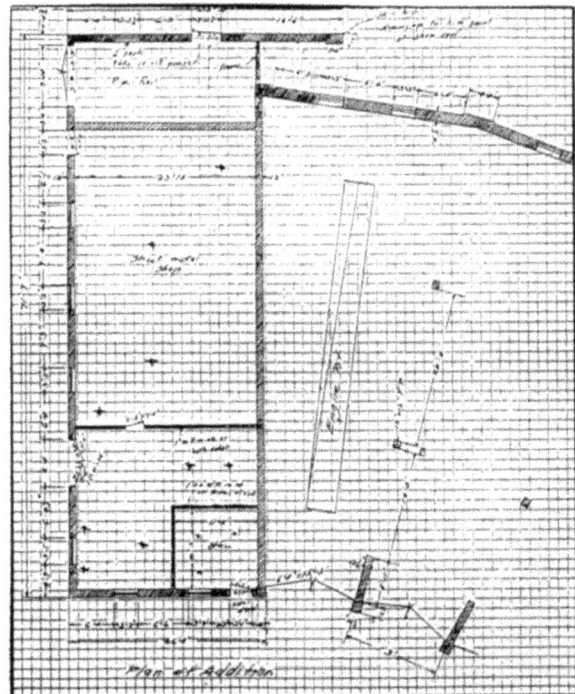

Plan of sheet metal shop that was annexed to building number 4. (National Records Center, Washington, D.C.)

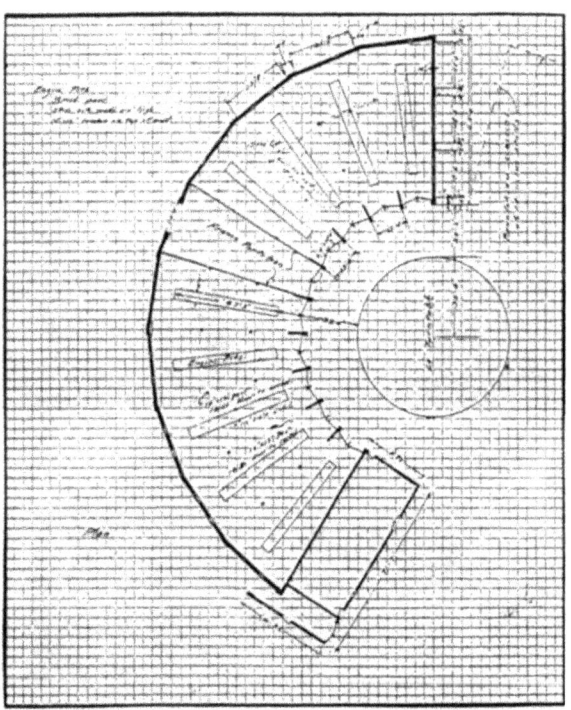

Plan of building number 4, formerly the south roundhouse, as it appeared in 1918. (National Records Center, Washington, D.C.)

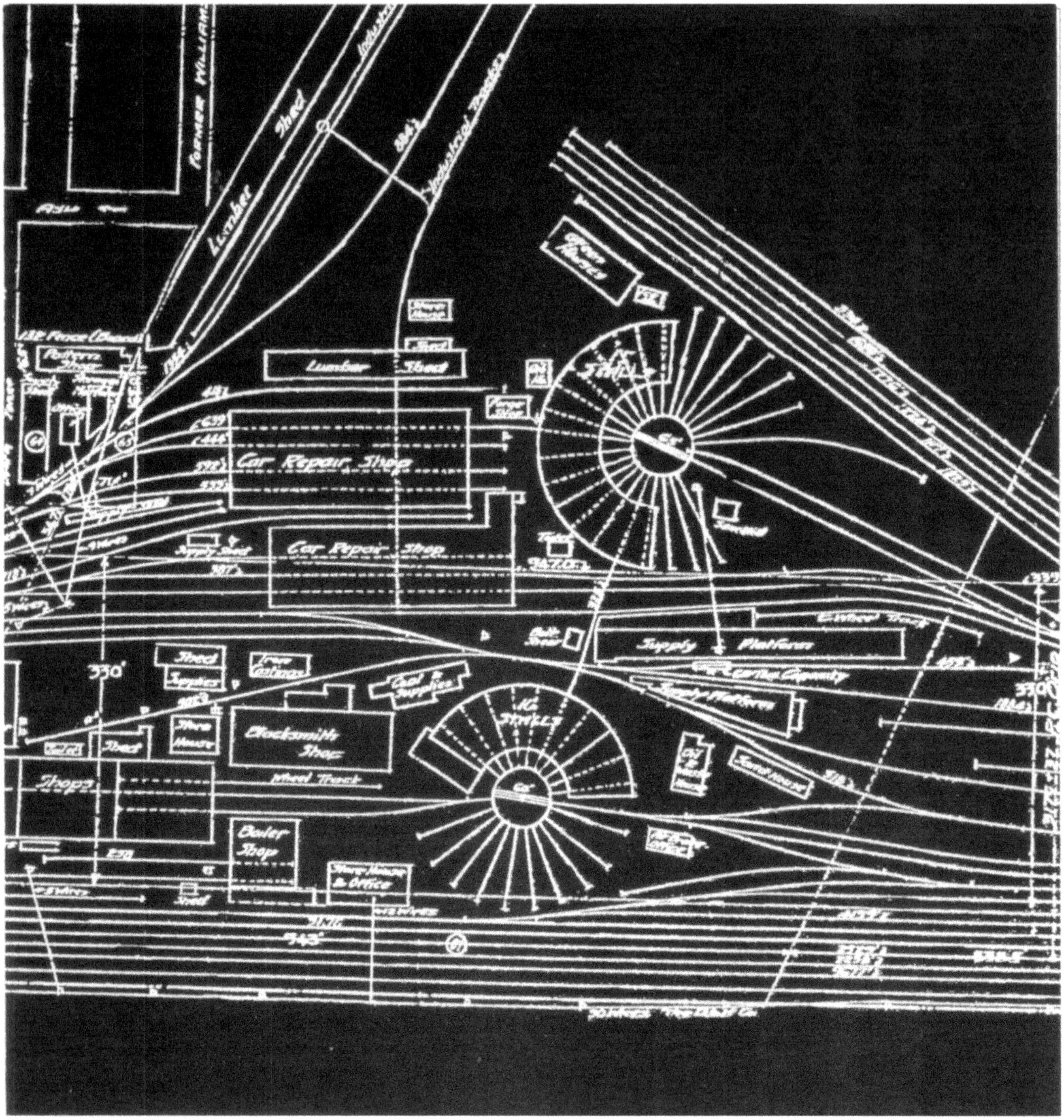

The original Oneonta Roundhouses and adjacent shop complex, circa 1918 (National Records Center, Washington, D.C.)

The remains of the north roundhouse are still visible in Oneonta Yards, 1992. (LRHS Collection)

CHAPTER 2

THE NEW ROUNDHOUSE

By the turn of the century, it had become painfully apparent that the Delaware and Hudson Railroad was in desperate need of more locomotive repair space at its Oneonta facility. When the D. & H. took over the Albany and Susquehanna in 1870, the company owned 35 locomotives. Thirty years later, in 1900, that number had grown to 165, but the two roundhouses at Oneonta provided a combined total of only 37 stalls. Not only was there a shortage of stalls but the existing ones were too short for the increasingly longer locomotives, making it impossible to close the doors behind them. The Delaware and Hudson management realized that they could no longer delay the construction of a new service facility and the first step toward addressing that problem was taken by the Company in the spring of 1904. It was at this time that the D. & H. purchased the properties belonging to John Sigsbee and Charles Bingham, which were located west of Fonda Avenue and north of the tracks. Nothing more was done on the project until April of 1905 when a delegation of Company officials, including President David Wilcox from New York City and Vice President/General Manager Abel I. Culver of Albany, visited Oneonta to inspect the potential site for the new roundhouse. Shortly after this visit, the company issued specifications for the new building in order to solicit construction bids from local contractors.

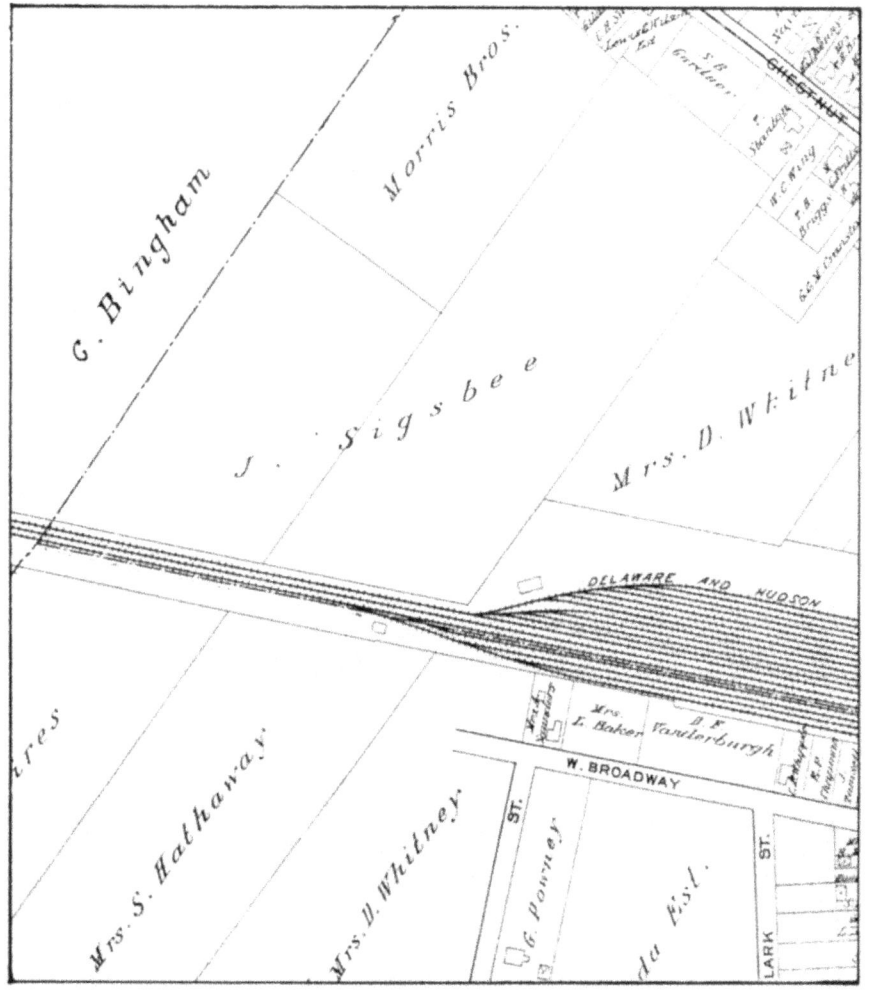

The future site of the new roundhouse as it appeared in 1903. (New Century Atlas of Otsego County, 1903)

The building specifications as issued by the company contained the following requirements: the building was to be of solid brick construction with gravel roof and contain a total of 52 stalls. The dimensions were to be as follows: 425 feet diameter with a turntable 75 feet long, with each stall 80 feet in length and each one with a drop pit. The building was to be heated with steam and the management projected a total construction budget of $100,000.00.

As the Company began looking at bids submitted, it became obvious that they would not be able to stay within their budget. The submissions from contractors were so high that the project was not even discussed at the Board of Managers meeting held in New York City on May 7, and the Chief Engineer's office in Albany notified the Oneonta Star that construction of the new roundhouse would be postponed indefinitely.

This seemed like very bad news for the village of Oneonta but within a month the outlook had changed dramatically. By early June crews were busy clearing brush from the roundhouse site and a sewer system was being installed to drain the surrounding swamp. It was also announced that a good deal of the building materials had already been purchased and that construction would begin before the 1st of July. The Company's Chief Engineer, James McMartin, explained that because satisfactory bids could not be obtained, the D. & H. had decided to construct most of the building with its own manpower. Several of the construction contracts were let to Albany firms; the building was designed by Howard Rogers, the roof was installed by James Ackroyd and the heating system by James Hunter, all of that city. All other work, with the exception of bricklaying, was performed by D. & H. employees under the supervision of Chief Engineer McMartin and Site Engineer J. F. Morgan.

Work on the building progressed rapidly and by the middle of July the entire site had been drained, filled and graded and crews were pouring the foundations. By the end of September all the pits and underground work had been finished and the contract for raising the brick superstructure had been let to Bennett and Butts of Oneonta, the only local contractor who was involved in the project. By the spring of 1906 the building was nearing completion and crews were putting the finishing touches on plumbing and wiring systems.

This drawing of the new roundhouse under construction was copied from a photograph in the May 1907 issue of Railway Engineering and Maintenance of Way that was not suitable for reproduction. The two workers in the foreground vividly illustrate the depth of foundation that was required due to the swampy terrain. (Railway Engineering and Maintenance of Way)

When the new roundhouse was opened in May of 1906, it stood as a structure of truly massive proportions, incorporating the latest innovations in locomotive maintenance and repair. The overall design of the building was strongly influenced by guidelines developed in 1902 by the American Railway Master Mechanics Association, which were put forth in a committee report entitled, "Arrangement and accessories of an up-to-date roundhouse."

Superior in size to any roundhouse previously constructed anywhere in the world, the building's diameter was 428 feet, with a circumference of 1,344 feet, over a quarter of a mile. It housed 1 3/4 miles of track, and its walls contained 1 1/2 million bricks. There were 52 stalls, each one 80 feet long, 4 of which had drop pits for changing driving wheels. An annex of 61 feet 6 inches by 108 feet 8 inches contained the machine shop, store house, boiler room, oil house and fan room. A toilet room, 27 feet by 28 feet 8 inches, was located near the machine shop and entered directly from the roundhouse.

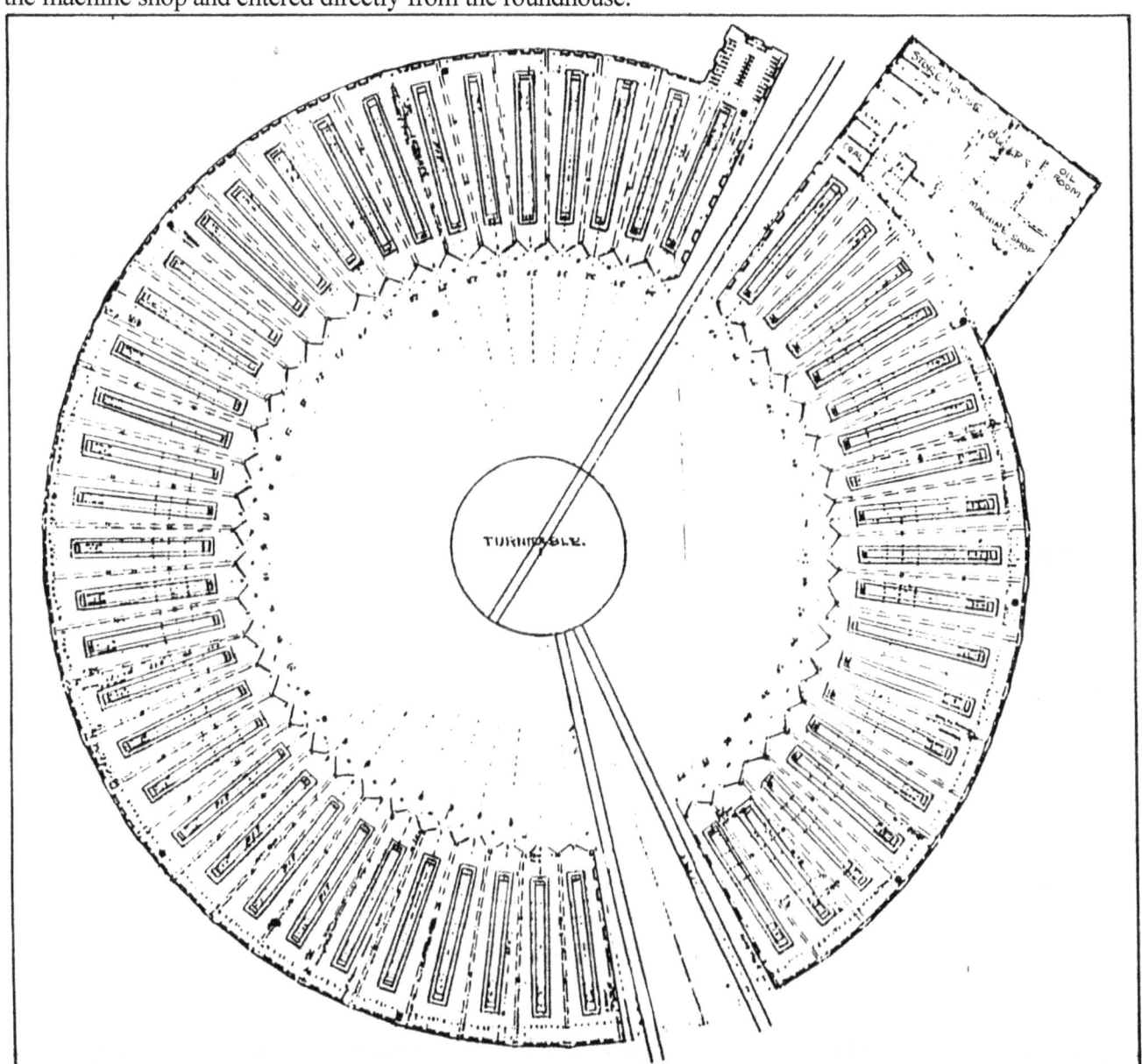

General plan of Oneonta Roundhouse showing arrangement of pits and location of machine shop and storeroom. (Railway Engineering and Maintenance of Way)

The turntable was 75 feet long, balanced and powered by an electric motor. Three tracks entered the roundhouse circle, two incoming and one outgoing, and a concrete cinder pit was constructed to serve both incoming tracks. The cinder pit consisted of two lateral trenches, each one 150 feet long by 12 feet wide by 18 inches deep on either side of a 5 foor deep pit which was equipped with two service tracks. Incoming locomotives would dump their ashes into one of the pits and, after cooling, the ashes would be raked into gondola cars which were positioned in the pit. The cinder pit was also equipped with eight 2 inch water bibs for hosing down locomotives. There were two water tanks adjacent to the cinder pit to service the incoming and outgoing locomotives.

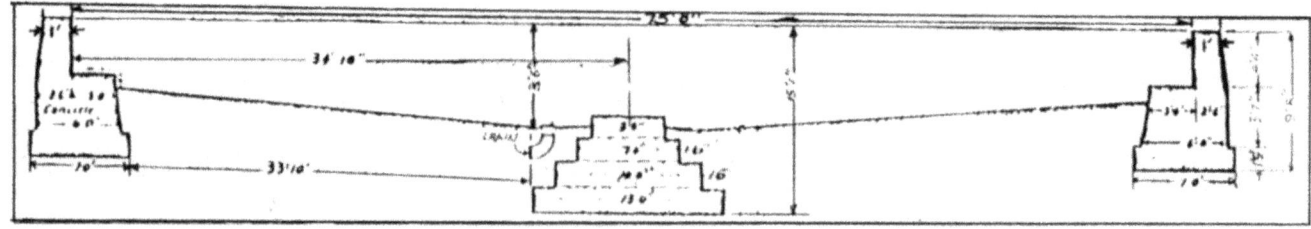

Section of turntable, Oneonta Roundhouse. (Railway Engineering and Maintenance of Way)

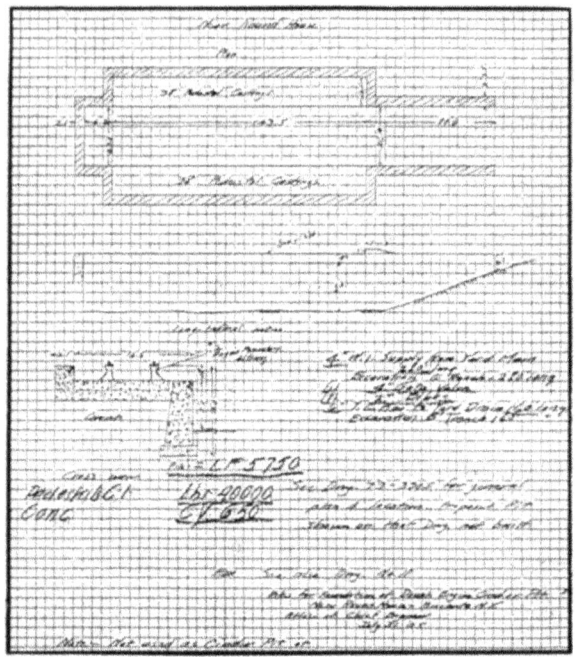

Plan and section of cinder pit, Oneonta Roundhouse. (National Records Center, Washington, D.C.)

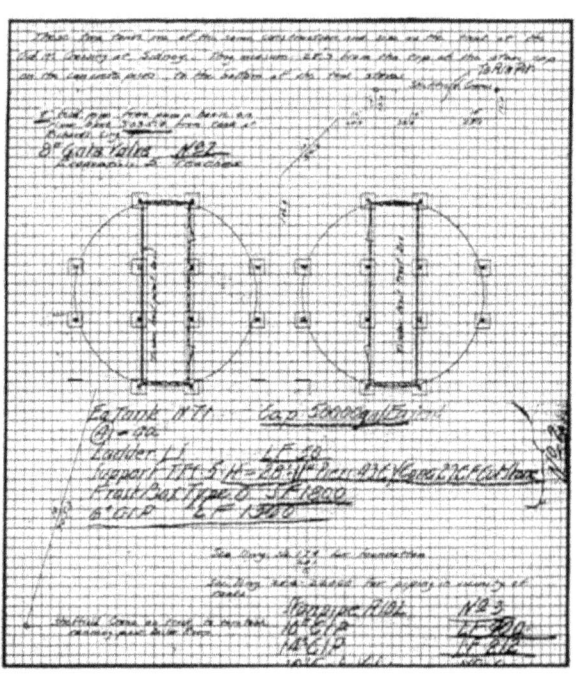

Plan of twin water tanks, Oneonta Roundhouse. (National Records Center, Washington, D.C.)

In construction, concrete was used for foundations, pits, conduits, floors and facing for the turntable pit. Brick was employed in the walls of all buildings and for a backing on the facing of the concrete drop pits. The roof was constructed of wood with 4 ply slag roofing and all skylights were of wire reinforced glass. Nearly all the beams, supports and braces were fabricated of wood rather than steel.

The interior height varied from 19 feet 4 inches to 21 feet 2 inches above the floor, and the skylights extended another 7 feet 6 inches above the roof. The skylights were 13 feet wide and located 26 feet 8 inches from the inside wall, providing excellent illumination for the cabs of locomotives. The smoke jacks were of the Dickinson adjustable type with an 8 foot flare on the lower end and located 20 feet from the outer wall.

The door posts were of cast-iron box sections, spaced 14 feet 6 inches from center to center, leaving a door opening of 13 feet 1 inch wide by 17 feet high. The doors were constructed from 1 1/2" by 3" pine, each hung on three heavy pin hinges.

There were 48 repair pits, each 58 feet 8 inches long and 4 feet wide, built entirely of concrete, with walls 20 inches thick on the sides and from 24 to 36 inches thick on the bottom. The floors of the pit were convex, the center being 3 inches higher than the sides and, longitudinally there was a drop of 12 inches toward the inner end for drainage. The rails were supported by a series of stone blocks 12 inches by 12 inches by 8 inches thick, set 3 feet apart and projecting 1 inch above the pit walls. Four tracks were arranged with drop pits for removing drive wheels, the pits being 6 feet deep by 6 feet 6 inches wide with walls 20 inches thick.

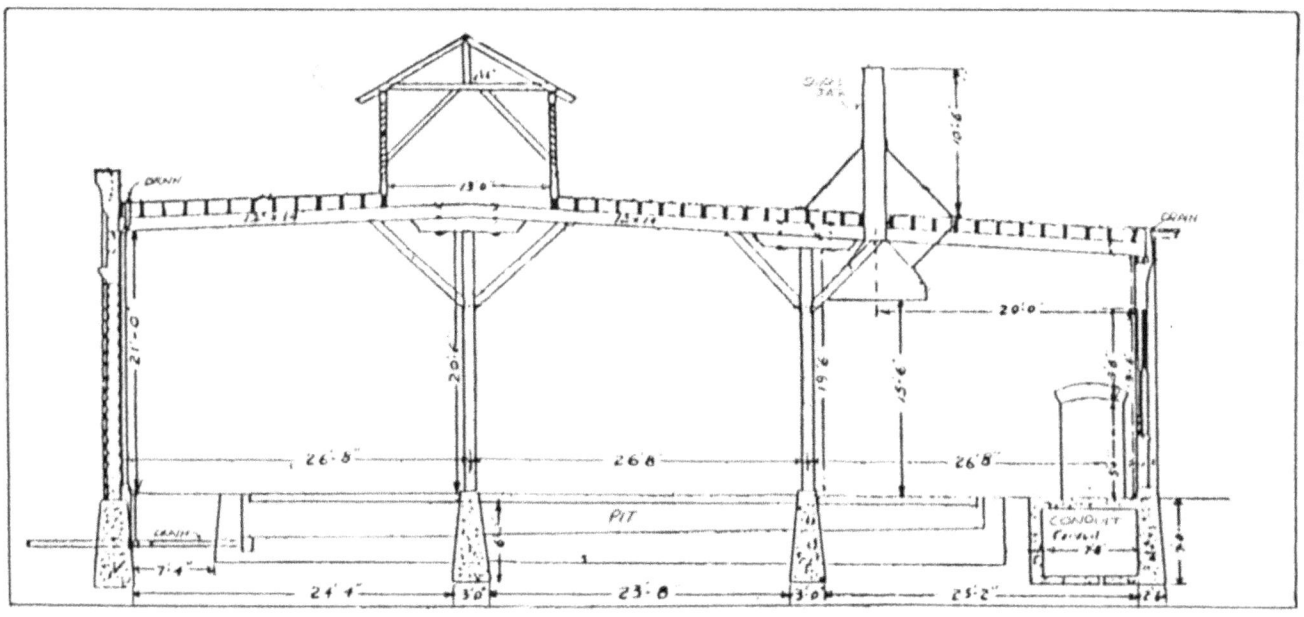

Section of Oneonta Roundhouse. (Railway Engineering and Maintenance of Way)

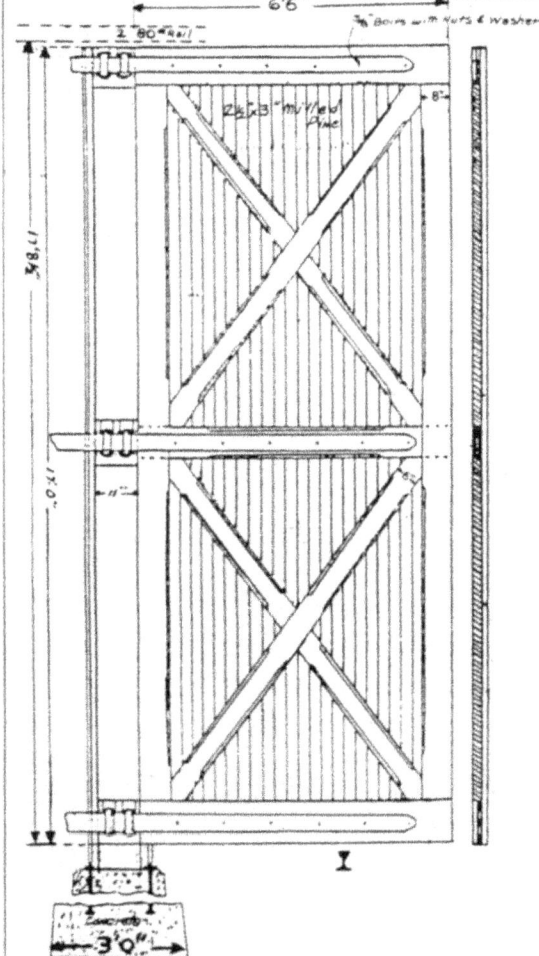

The building was heated with a hot blast ventilating system which also cooled in the summer. The system was manufactured by the Pittsburgh Stoker Company and consisted of a steel plate fan 10 feet in diameter which delivered 103 c.f.m. at 140 r.p.m. The fan discharged directly into the heating conduit which traveled the circumference of the building. The heating conduit consisted of a rectangular channel which used the foundation of the roundhouse for its outer wall and provided support for the floor with 12 inch I-beams and 80 pound steel rails. At the point where the fan discharged into the conduit, its dimensions were 5 feet 6 inches high by 7 feet 8 inches wide. The conduit tapered in both directions and, at 180 degrees from the fan, it narrowed to 3 feet high by 2 feet 6 inches wide, at which point there was a damper. Between the pits were 18 inch cast iron pipes running off the main conduit which branched into two 12 inch pipes that delivered air to the adjacent pits.

Plan and section of door, Oneonta Roundhouse. (Railway Engineering and Maintenance of Way)

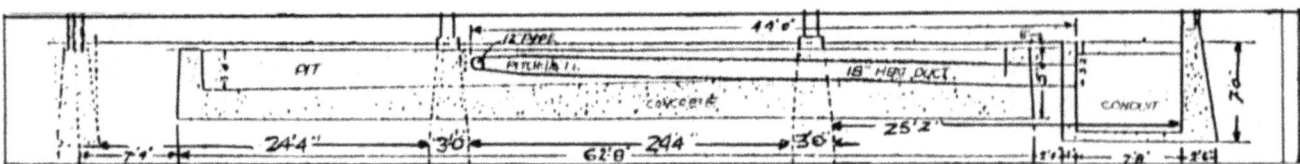

Longitudinal section of repair pit, showing heating conduit. (Railway Engineering and Maintenance of Way)

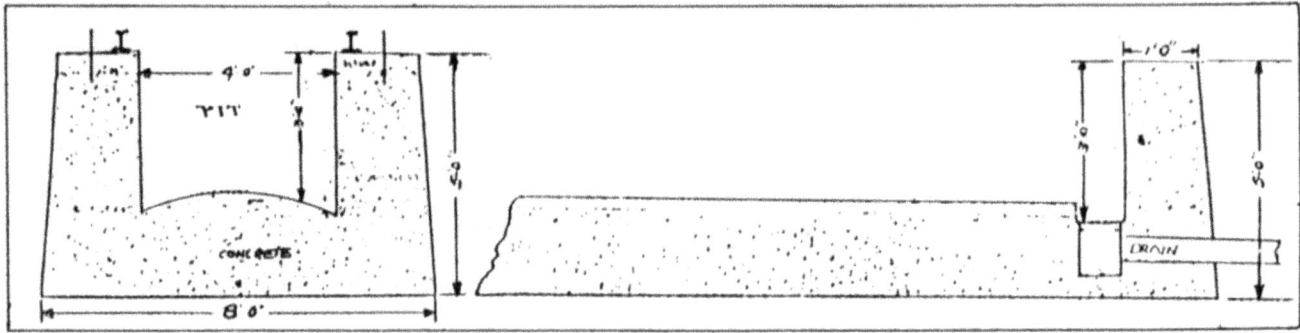

Longitudinal transverse and section of repair pit showing drainage system. (Railway Engineering and Maintenance of Way)

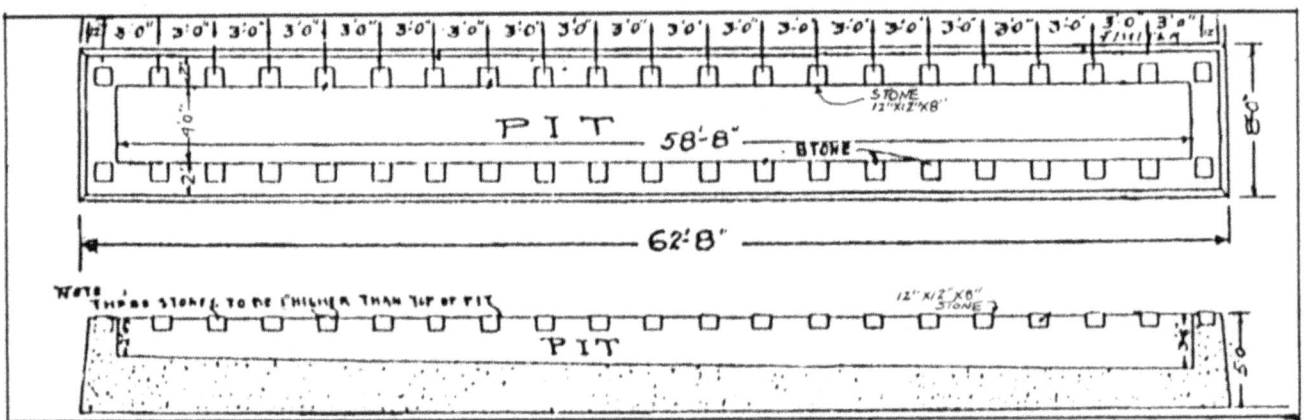

Plan and longitudinal section of repair pit. (Railway Engineering and Maintenance of Way)

Drainage was accomplished through a system of iron and vitrified piping running from the building to a nearby creek. A 4 inch drain pipe was laid from each pit to a 12 inch line laid in a circle of 108 feet radius from the center of the turntable pit. Four inch pipes drained the roof while 8 inch pipes were laid from the turntable pit, machine shop and toilet room to the 12 inch pipe around the turntable, which in turn entered a 24 inch main that emptied into the creek. There were 10 manholes to access the heating conduit and 7 manholes to access the drainage system.

Water was supplied from a well consisting of ten 2 inch pipes driven 25 feet into the ground, coupled together at the surface and fed into a 6 inch Worthington pump which furnished 450,000 gallons of water every 24 hours. Two 80,000 gallon tanks were constructed for storage and supplying engines direct. The roundhouse was supplied with a 6 inch pipe running through the conduit, which fed into a 4 inch distribution pipe which in turn fed two 2 inch laterals between every two pits.

The coal storage room was adjacent to the boiler room and had a capacity of 152 tons. A standard gauge track extended the length of the room enabling coal to be handled directly from the cars to the boilers. The boiler room housed three tubular boilers, each rated at 152 horsepower. The boilers were built by the Franklin Boiler Works of Troy, New York.

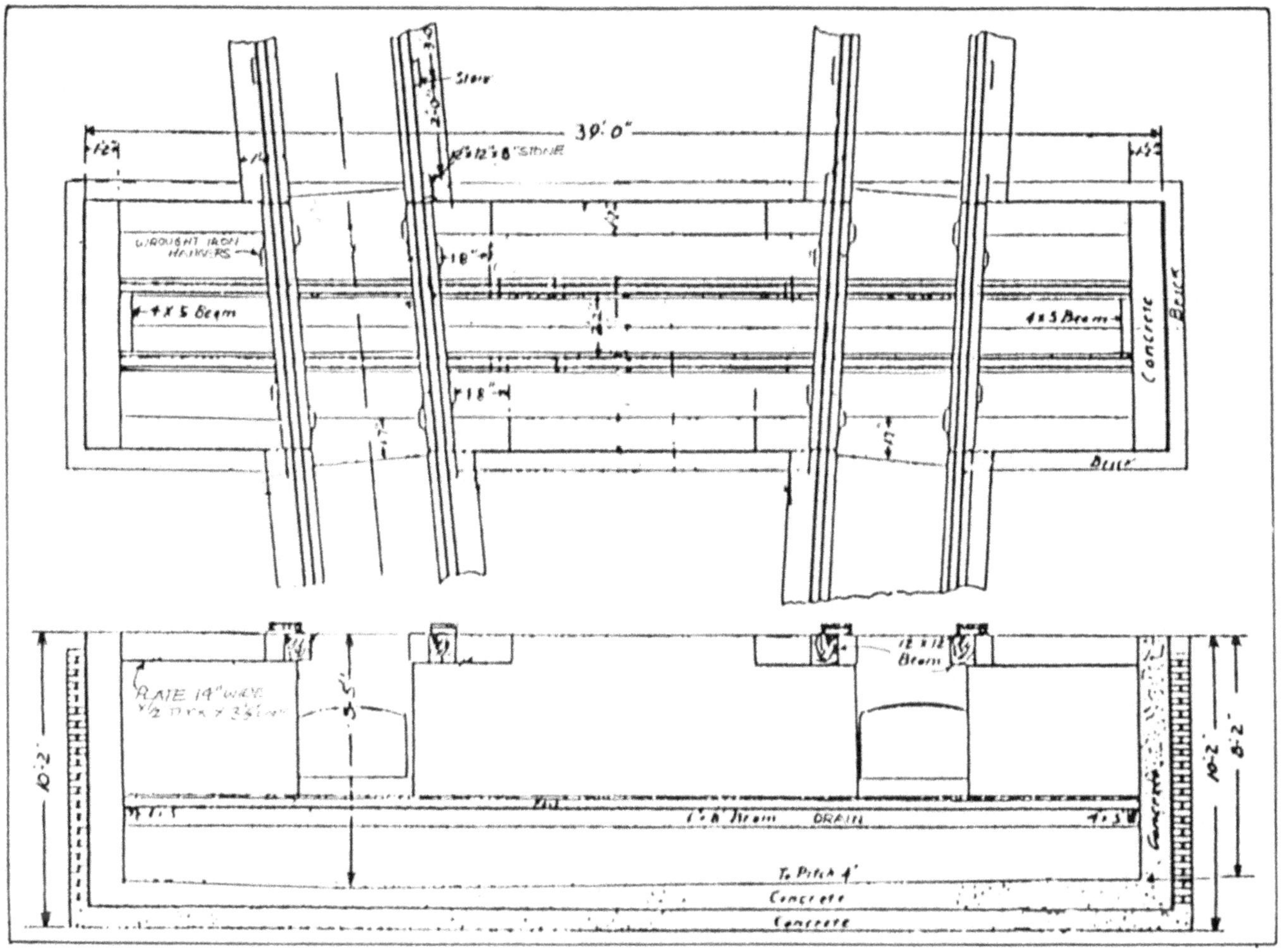

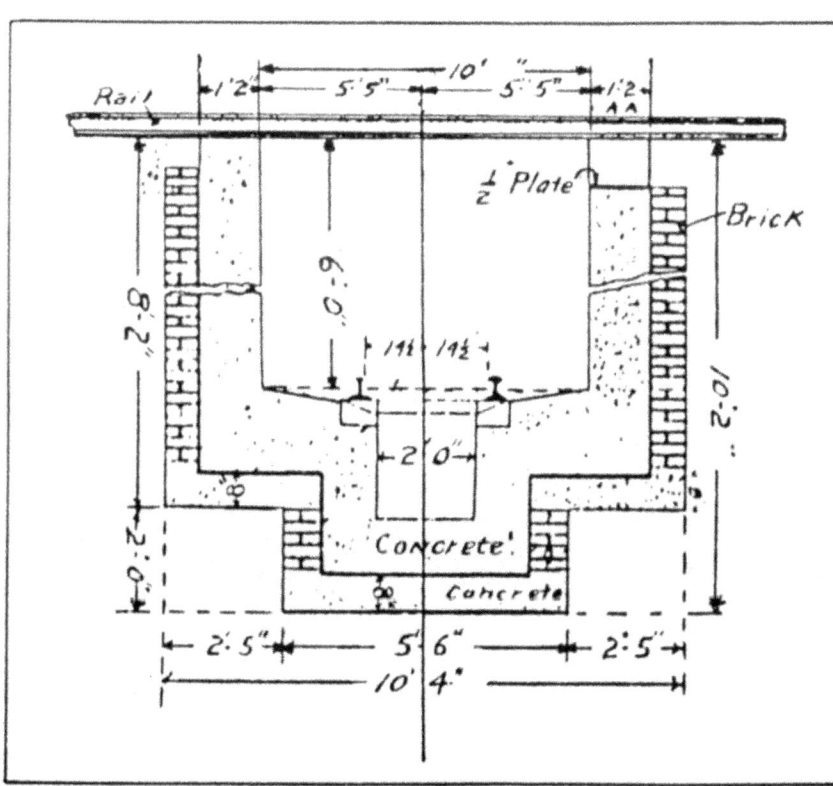

Plan and longitudinal section of drop pit, Oneonta Roundhouse. (Railway Engineering and Maintenance of Way)

The fan room, machine shop and storeroom were directly adjacent to each other and the roundhouse. The storeroom contained five submerged oil tanks, one of 2,000 gallon capacity and four of 1,500 gallon capacity. The Bowser System of oil distribution was used in the storeroom, with oil being pumped to a dispensing station as needed.

Transverse section of drop pit. (Railway Engineering and Maintenance of Way)

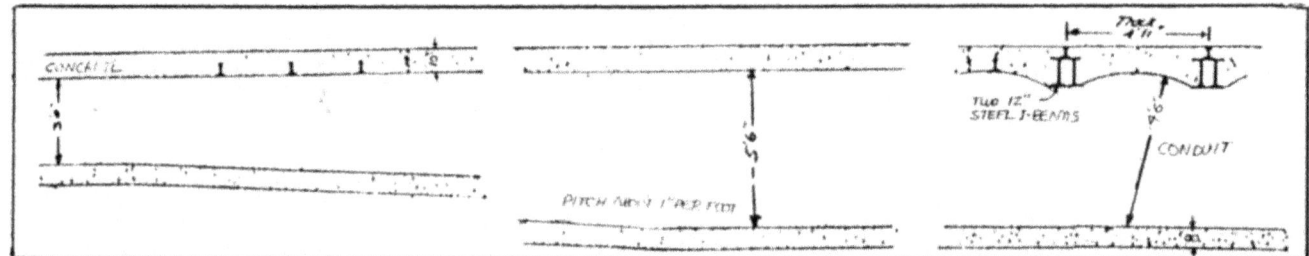

Longitudinal section through heating conduit, showing method of reinforcing. (Railway Engineering and Maintenance of Way)

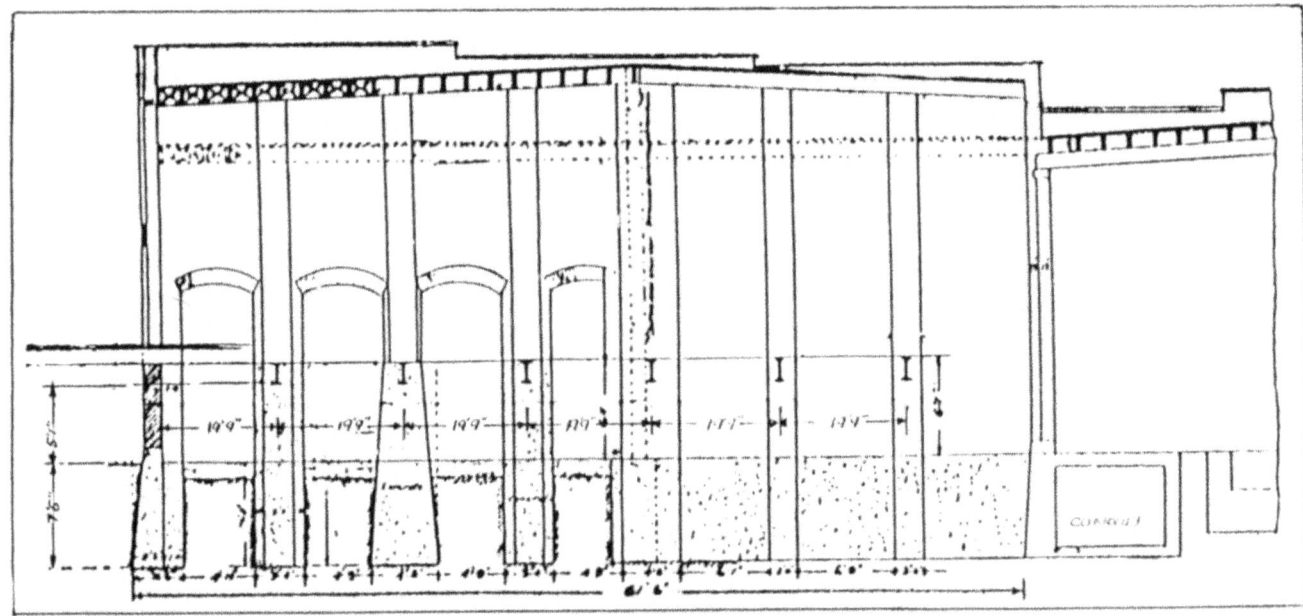

Section through coal storage room, showing concrete piers and I-beam supports for trestle. (Railway Engineering and Maintenance of Way)

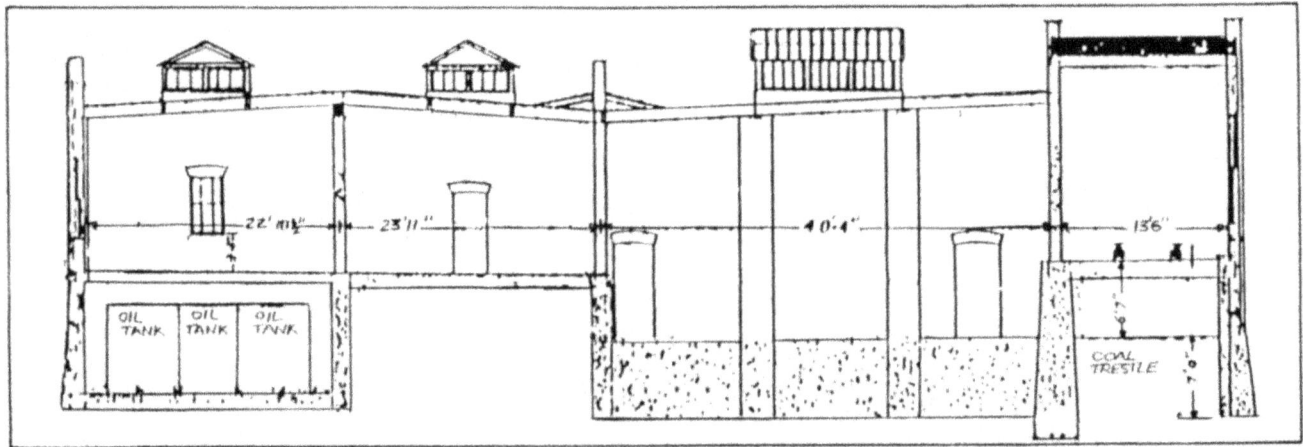

Cross section of annex showing arrangement of tanks, construction of building and elevated coal trestle. (Railway Engineering and Maintenance of Way)

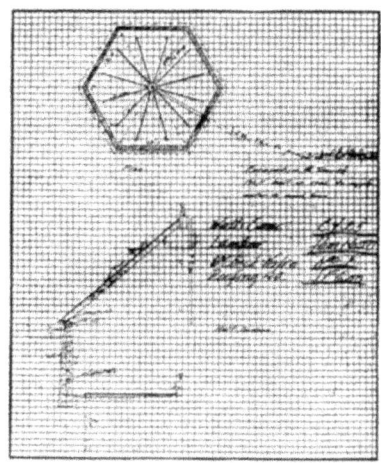 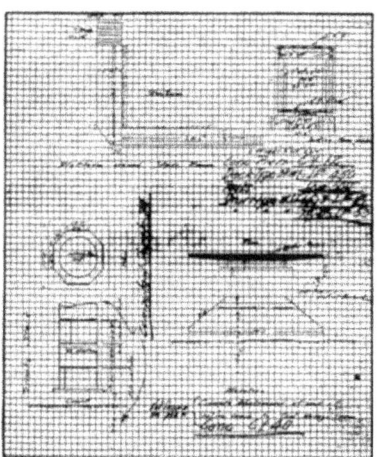 

Arrangement of wells and pump, Oneonta Roundhouse. (National Records Center, Washington, D.C.)

Detail of smokestack and storeroom platform, Oneonta Roundhouse. (National Records Center, Washington, D.C.)

Detail of pump house adjacent to coal storage room. (National Records Center, Washington, D.C.)

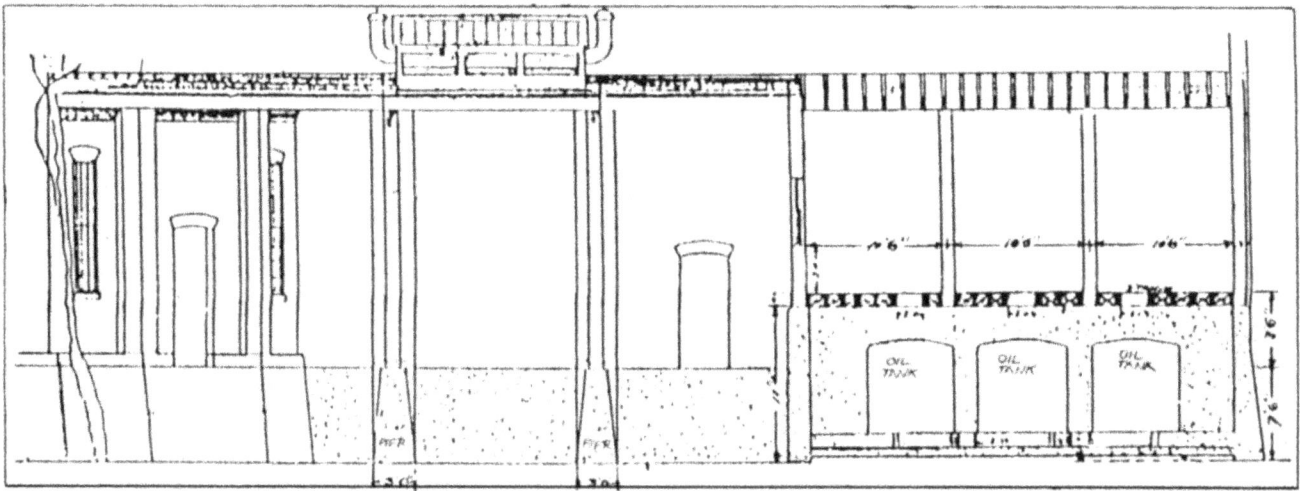

Section through storeroom and oil house, showing construction and concrete foundation. (Railway Engineering and Maintenance of Way)

The new roundhouse, nearly $50,000.00 over budget when completed, was formally inspected and accepted by the Company in August of 1906, thereby bestowing upon Oneonta the distinction of hosting the largest roundhouse in the world, a claim that went unchallenged for over a quarter of a century.

Shortly after the roundhouse was completed, a coal trestle was erected 500 feet south of the building, along with a combination coal and sand pocket and a sand dryer. In addition, a wood frame blacksmith shop was built adjacent to the beating plant and a small tool shed was installed between the two incoming tracks.

Once in operation, the Oneonta Roundhouse became the model of an efficient locomotive facility. Engines entering the complex followed a very ordered sequence of procedures: The first stop would be the coal pocket where the tender would be filled and sand would be taken on. Next would be the ash pit where the front end of the fire would be dumped into one of the concrete trenches. The fire would then be raked back, all the while maintaining a boiler pressure of 200 p.s.i. Finally the engine would be hosed down and take on water from one of the storage tanks.

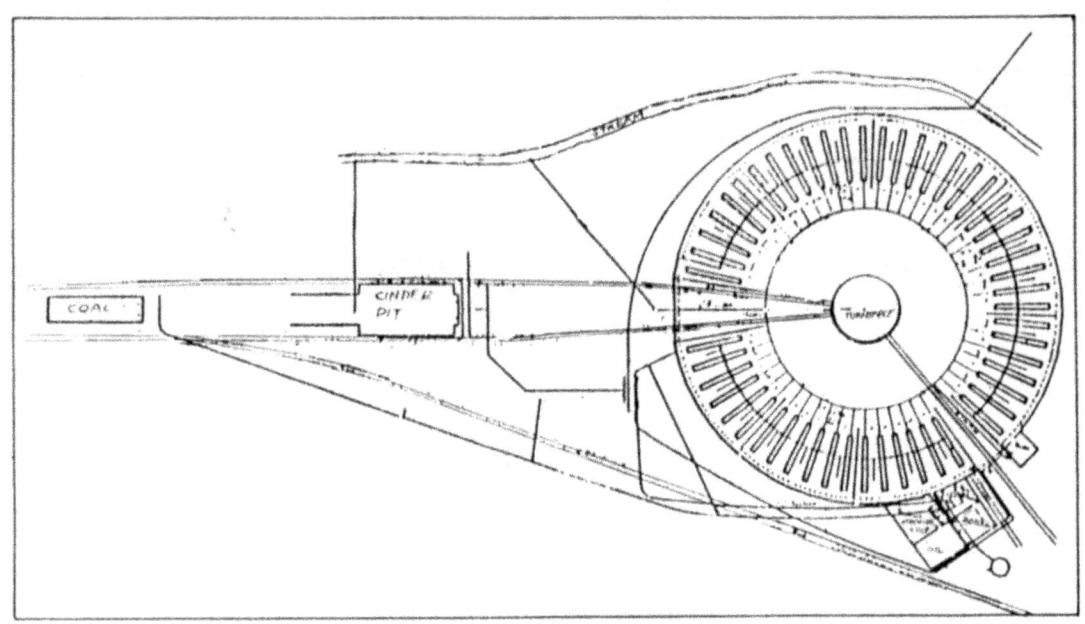

General layout of locomotive terminal, Oneonta, New York. (Railway Engineering and Maintenance of Way)

This postcard view of the Oneonta Roundhouse was taken from Chestnut Street, looking south, in 1906. The smoke on the left side of the building indicates one of the Dickinson smoke jacks is in use. Note the lack of development around River Street, an area that would see a major housing boom in the next few years. (Mrs. Wilmer Bresee)

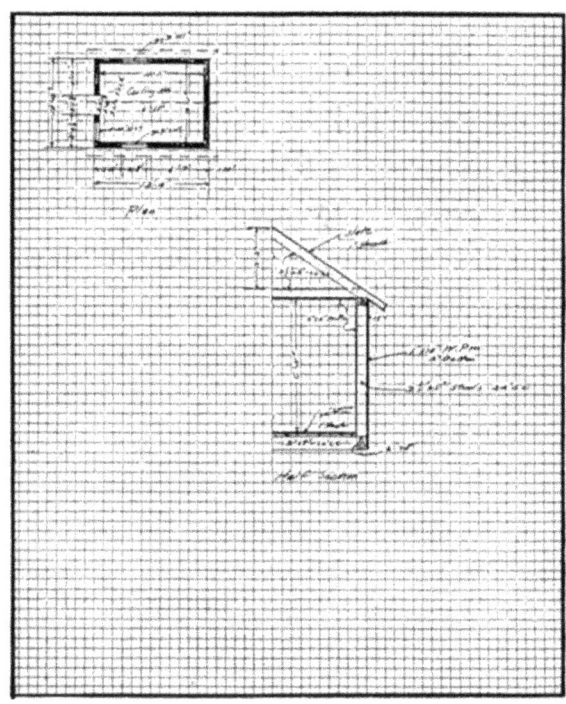

Plan and elevation of coal pocket boiler house, Oneonta Engine Facility. (National Records Center, Washington, D.C.)

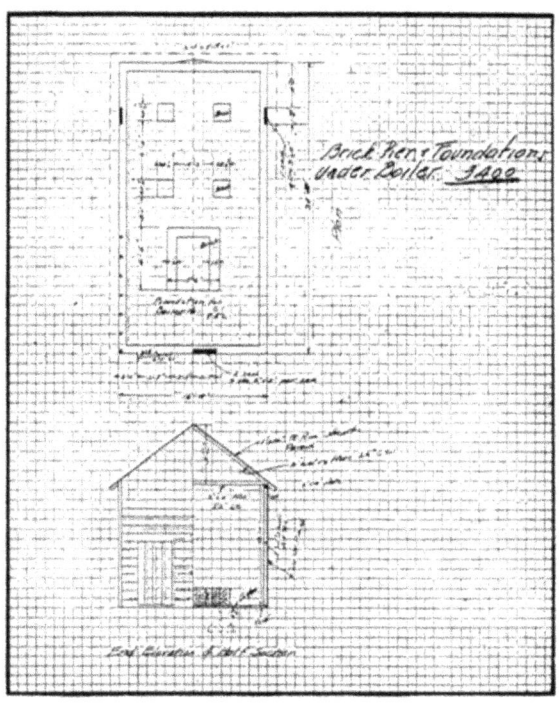

Plan and section of coal storage foreman's office, Oneonta Engine Facility. (National Records Center, Washington, D.C.)

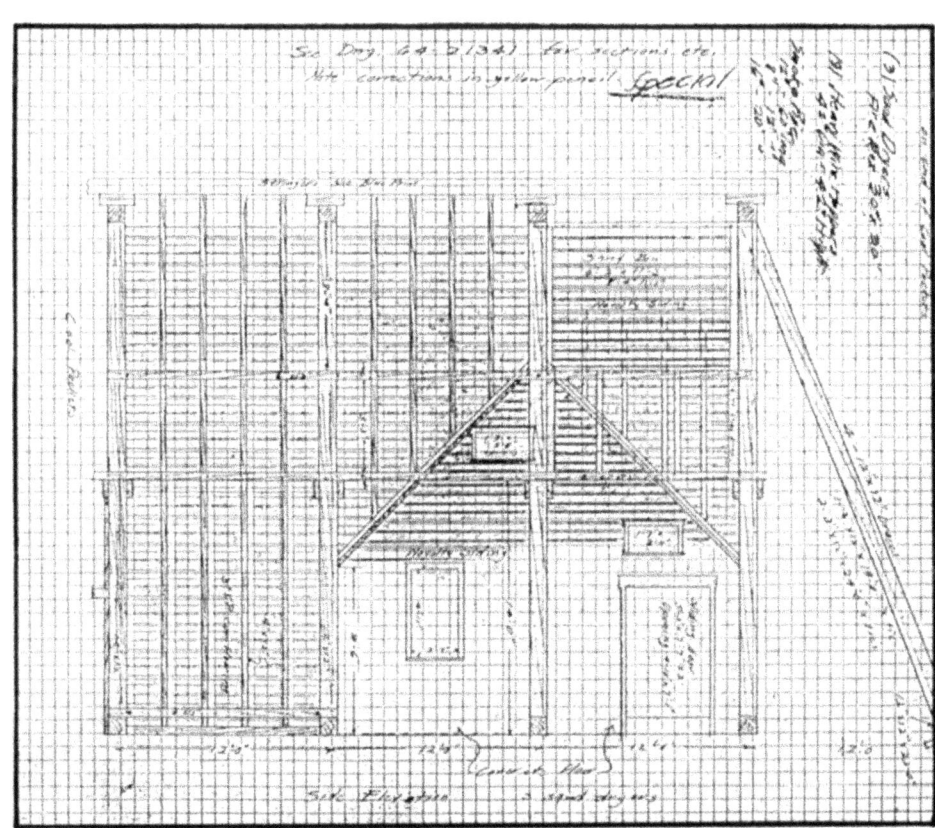

Construction detail of sand house, Oneonta Engine Facility. (National Records Center, Washington, D.C.)

If the engineer was experiencing any problems with the locomotive, he would make out a slip which would be forwarded to the appropriate repair department. Each time a power unit was brought into the roundhouse, it was thoroughly inspected to detect any problems the engineer might not be aware of.

The hostler was provided with a roster that directed him in locating engines into the correct stalls and if a locomotive was not on the roster, it would be placed in one of the available stalls for inspection.

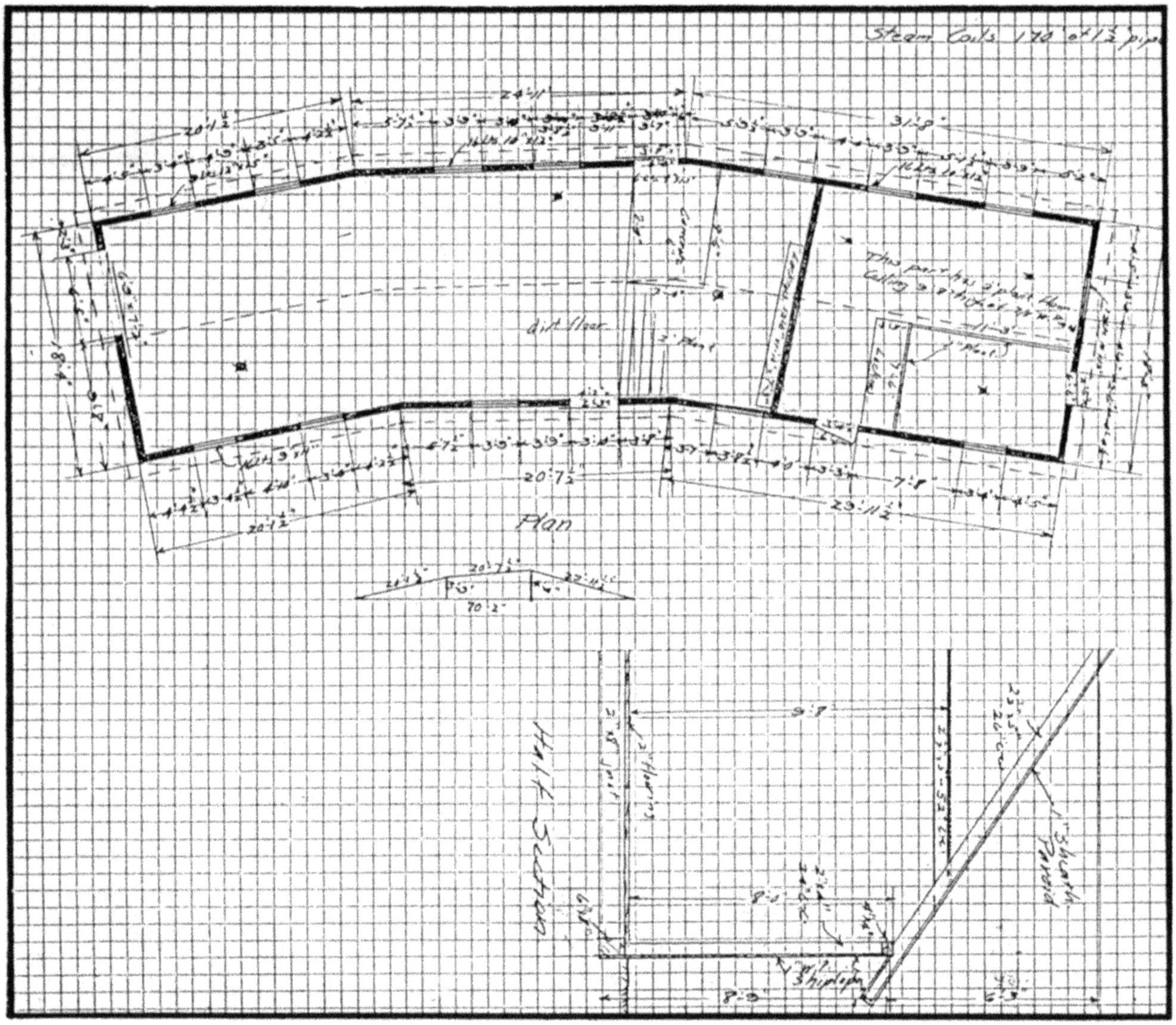

Plan and section of blacksmith shop, Oneonta Roundhouse. (National Records Center, Washington, D.C.)

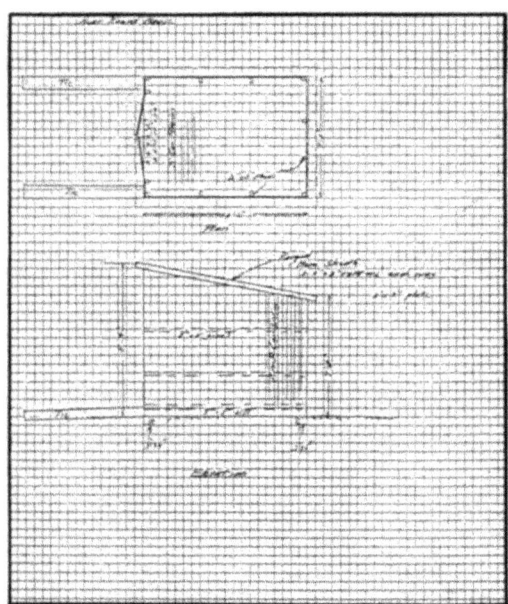

Fire hose house, Oneonta Roundhouse. (National Records Center, Washington, D.C.)

Working at the roundhouse, like all railroad labor, was extremely hazardous. The first fatality at the new building occurred on January 11, 1908. Charles W. Wildenstien, a day hostler for the D. & H., was found dead under the turntable at 8:30 P.M. Mr. Wildenstien was a veteran of six years with the Company, having been a native of Wayne County, Pennsylvania. He relocated to Oneonta in 1902 and took up residence with the Hubbell family on lower Chestnut Street.

After the discovery had been made, workmen set about the unpleasant task of extricating Mr. Wildenstien's body from the turntable machinery. It was estimated that he had been entangled in the mechanism for over an hour and a half and that at least 14 locomotives had been moved during that time period.

Investigators later pieced together the chain of events that led up to the worker's horrible death. Apparently Mr. Wildenstien went off duty about 7 P.M. and had hitched a ride on the tender of an engine heading out of the complex. While on the turntable platform, the lid fell off his lunch pail and he climbed down into the pit to retrieve it. While searching for the lid, he came in contact with some of the electrical cables that powered the table and was frozen by the current passing through his body. Mr. Wildenstien's electrocution shorted the power connections on the table, making it inoperable. The impatient operator, not checking to ascertain the cause of the malfunction, summoned help to turn the table by hand. And so the victim's lifeless body was hopelessly mangled by the table's gears and trucks as it was rotated manually.

Although no charges were filed relative to the death of Charles Wildenstien, a Company directive was issued immediately, requiring anyone entering the turntable pit to notify the cabin operator in advance.

The Oneonta Roundhouse, looking north, 1906. the postcard company was off by 28 feet on the building's diameter. (Author's collection)

The construction of the new roundhouse had a dramatic impact on the welfare of Oneonta. In January of 1906 it was announced that the Delaware and Hudson had engaged in large purchases of land in the village's west end in order to allow for a major expansion of the yard complex. All land purchases were negotiated by George I. Wilber, who sat on the Company's Board of Managers and oversaw all real estate transactions for the Oneonta facility. The purchases gave the Company title to all the property between Fonda Avenue and Richard's Crossing, as far south as the Susquehanna River. The combined parcels totaled over 350 acres and the D. & H. management announced that the Oneonta yards would be developed into the main distribution center for the entire system.

In this photo of the new Oneonta Roundhouse taken in 1906, the wash crew can be seen hosing down the Mother Hubbard on the left side of the pit, while another work gang is waiting for the ashes to cool so they can be transferred to the waiting gondolas. (Author's collection).

This photograph of the new Roundhouse was taken shortly after the building was put into use in May of 1906. The frame building to the left of the entrance was the Master Mechanic's office. The depression in the middle foreground was the original ash pit and wash rack. The lumber for the blacksmith shop has been stacked to the right of the twin water towers, while the smokestack is nearing completion in the background. Directly below the Master Mechanic's office, a string of cinder cars is waiting to be unloaded to fill in the swamp. (Mrs. Minnie Bell)

The rapid expansion of the shop facilities involved the hiring of hundreds of additional workers, which in turn generated an urgent need for new housing in the village and a construction boom in the west end soon followed. During June of 1906, the Shearer Real Estate Company purchased several tracts of land in the 6th ward, laid out streets and sold off lots to the newly arrived railroaders and their families. In addition to extending Miller and Gilbert Streets, two new thoroughfares, Park and Riverview were surveyed and quickly settled.

The population boom initiated by the new roundhouse continued through the next decade, with the village experiencing a 32% population growth increase between 1900 and 1910, from 7,147 to 9,491.

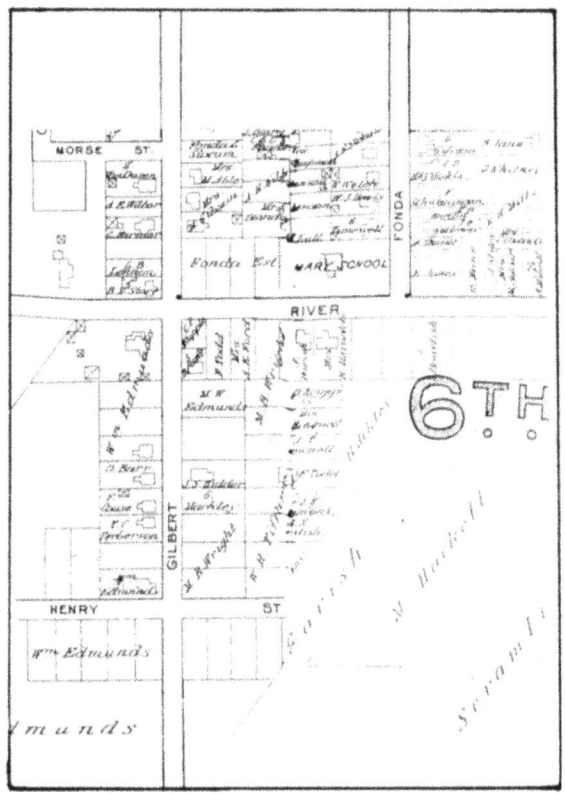 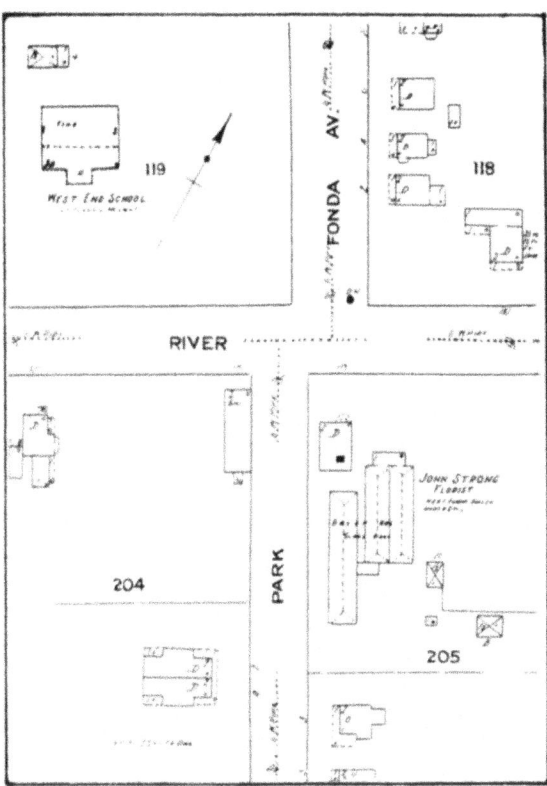

The two maps above clearly illustrate the development that took place in Oneonta after the new roundhouse was opened in 1906. The map on the left, drawn in 1903, shows Fonda Avenue terminating at River Street. The map on the right was drawn in 1910, four years after the roundhouse had been opened. By this time Park Avenue had been opened, and a florist shop and several residences had been constructed. (New Century Atlas of Otsego County, 1903; Sanborn Insurance Map Atlas of Oneonta, 1910)

CHAPTER THREE

IMPROVEMENTS

The first repair work performed on the new roundhouse took place on March 14, 1907. This work was made necessary because of damages inflicted when a loaded car was backed through the wall of the building. In the summer of 1907, the Company established a lunch room adjacent to the roundhouse, which also included sleeping booths for the purpose of allowing crews from other points on the system to obtain needed rest and nourishment while waiting for orders.

The first actual improvements at the facility were made in 1908. The northeast was stricken with a severe drought that year and by August Oneonta had been without any appreciable rainfall for over three months. The city was forced to enact emergency conservation measures, with fines being imposed for unnecessary waste.

As the crisis worsened, the city was faced with a very difficult decision; the largest consumer of municipal water was the D. & H. shop complex and the choice had to be made whether to supply the Company yards or the households of Oneonta. Pursuing the humane option, the city crews turned off the shop mains in mid August, thereby forcing the Railroad to fall back on its system of driven wells and a small pond, which were already severely depleted.

This action by the city, although unavoidable, threw the shops into temporary chaos. Huge quantities of water were vital to steam locomotive operation and the Company's supply was totally inadequate for its needs. In desperation, the old water tank adjacent to the depot was restored and two pumps were pressed into service pumping water from the mill race. The pumps were powered by steam from a stationary engine mounted on a flat car near the ice house.

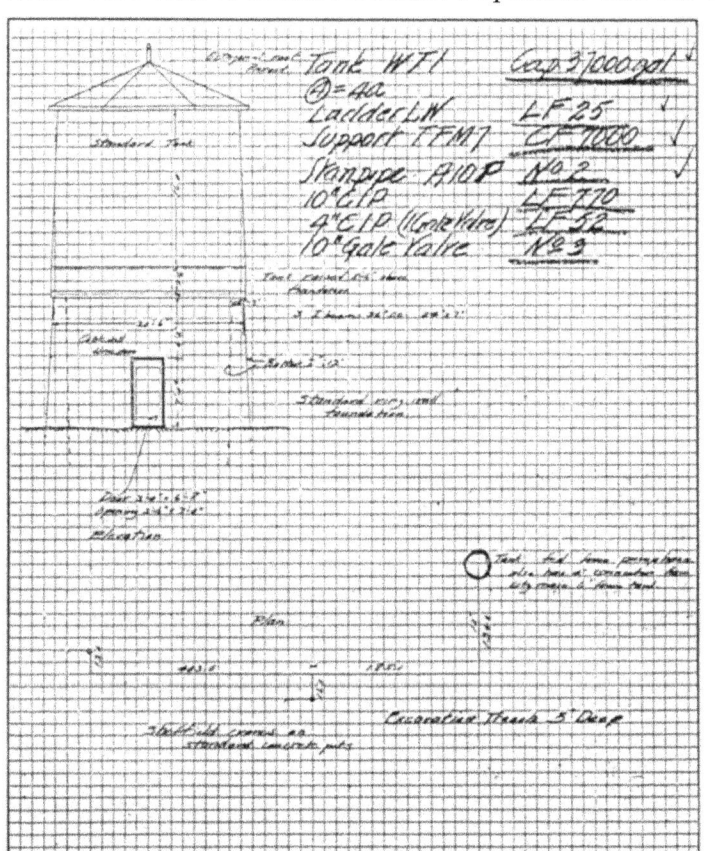

The greatest crisis facing the facility was the lack of a sufficient supply of water for the roundhouse complex. Attempting to deal with the emergency as quickly as possible, crews were put to work laying above-ground mains from the roundhouse to the Susquehanna River and a temporary track was installed to the pumping site. A locomotive was then moved into position to furnish power for pumps which would transport water to the building mains.

The drawing shows the water tower near the passenger depot that was pressed into service during the drought of 1908. (National Records Center, Washington, D.C.)

35

This measure alleviated the water shortage to some degree but, because the pumps were constantly in service, there were continual breakdowns. This situation led to lost time for employees who had to be sent home when the lines went dry. In order to supplement the temporary pumping station, the Company engaged in drilling additional wells on their property. By September the yard was pumping water from 31 wells but was still unable to meet its demand.

In October of 1908 the Company Directors held a special meeting to deal with the ongoing water supply problem at the Oneonta Yards. It was agreed that a long term solution was needed and, after deliberation, the decision was made to construct a permanent pumping station on the Susquehanna River. A site was chosen near Richard's Crossing and construction began shortly after the 1st of November. The station was completed and put into use in December of 1908, thereby enabling the Company to maintain its own water supply, independent of the city mains.

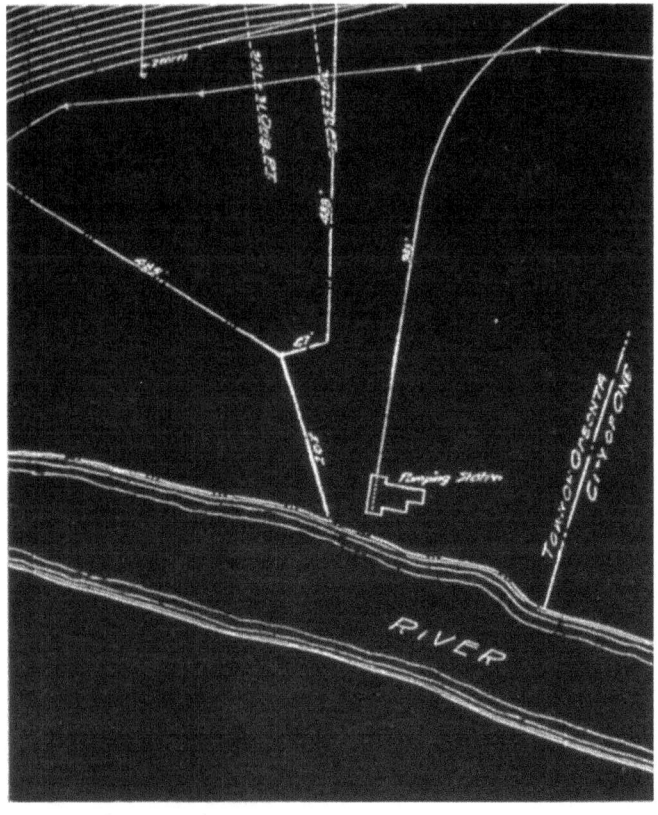

Company drawing of the pumping station that was erected in 1908 by the Delaware and Hudson to eliminate the shortage of water at the Oneonta Shops. (LRHS Collection)

A great deal of concern was aroused in Oneonta when it was made known in the summer of 1912 that the D. & H. was planning an extensive enlargement of its Watervliet Shops, a move which would possibly include the transfer of many employees from the Oneonta facility. In order to alleviate this concern, the Company announced plans for major improvements at the Oneonta Roundhouse complex. In August of that year, crews were surveying the property below the coal trestle for new ash pits which would be large enough to handle the increased locomotive traffic at the facility. The first pit was completed in April of 1913 and the second pit was completed in August of that year. Designed for efficient operation and maximum capacity, each pit was 170 feet long and 15 feet wide and contained 12 feet of water. Incoming locomotives would dump their ashes into the water where they were cooled and then picked up by overhead cranes to be dumped into gondola cars. Once the new ash pits were put into use, the old cinder pit just below the roundhouse was used solely for washing locomotives.

The Company also announced in the fall of 1912 plans to install a new power plant to handle the increased demand at the facility, brought on in part by the new ash pit cranes. This project involved the installation of two new 400 horsepower boilers which were capable of a combined output of 2,500 kilowatts. In addition, two new boilers of 2,500 horsepower each were installed at the roundhouse to handle future needs at that location.

In order to provide sufficient draft for the new boilers, the Company contracted the General Concrete Company of Chicago to construct a new smokestack which was to be 160 feet high, 50 feet higher than the existing stack. Under the direction of general foreman J. G. Prewett, ground was broken on the project on May 12, 1913. The excavation for the base of the structure measured 21 feet by 21 feet by 9 1/2 feet deep. Piles were sunk in the swampy soil to support the immense weight of the stack.

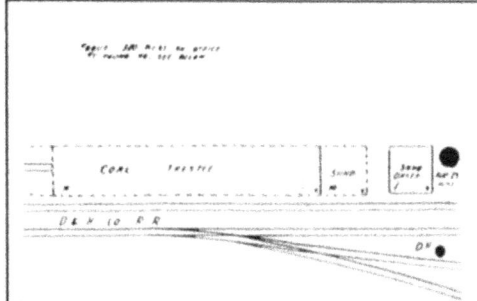

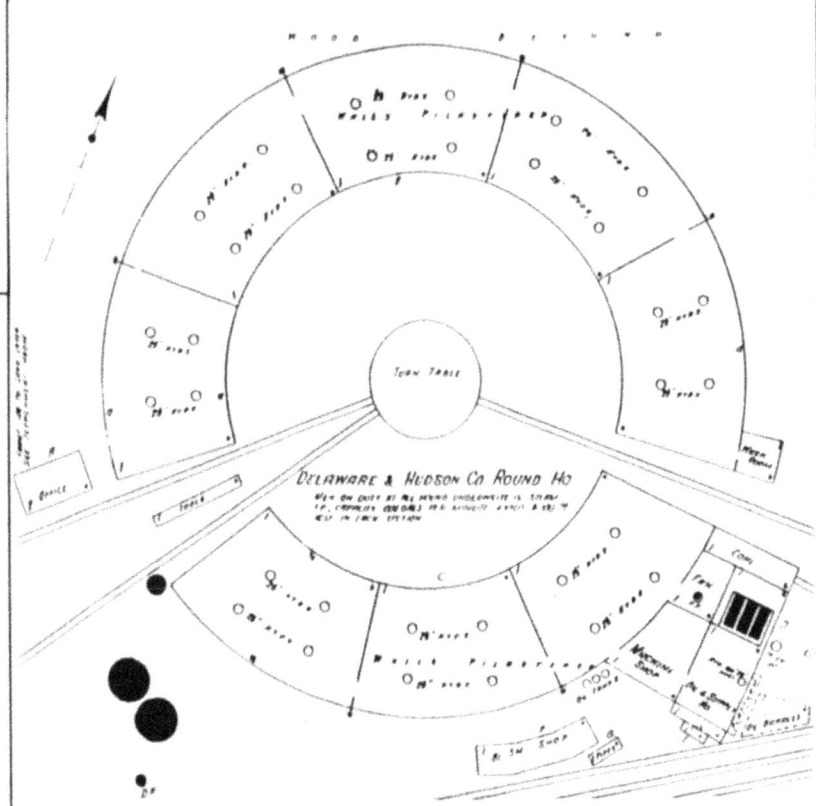

The Oneonta Roundhouse as it appeared in 1910. The tool shed between the two incoming tracks was assembled from two car bodies placed end to end, and was installed in 1907 and taken down about 1913. The wood frame blacksmith shop below the roundhouse was erected in 1906 and dismantled in 1927. The inset details the combination coaling and sanding plant that was installed in 1906. (Sanborn Insurance Map Atlas of Oneonta, 1910)

Company drawing showing the new ash pits which were installed in 1913, and their relative location to the rest of the facility. (Chris Whiteman)

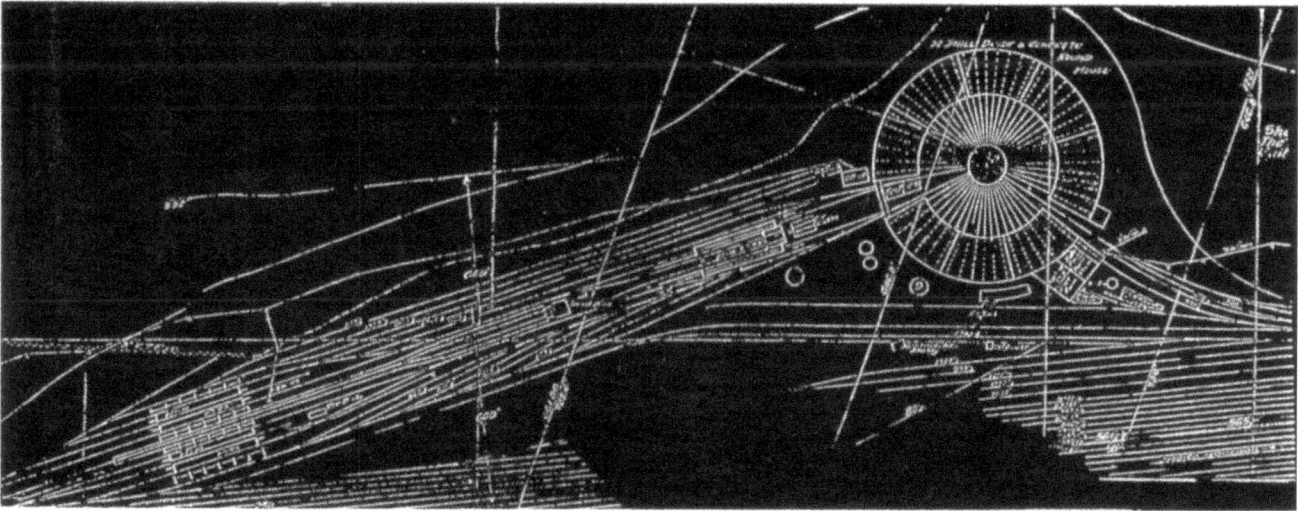

The stack was completed on July 12, 1913, having been constructed entirely of concrete with steel wire mesh reinforcing. It measured 12 feet 6 inches outside diameter at the base and 10 feet 6 inches outside diameter at the top, and 10 feet 8 inches inside diameter at the base and 8 feet inside diameter at the top. The inside of the flue was lined with firebrick for the first 50 feet. Once the stack was completed, it was faced with brick and a lightning protection system was installed by the Carl Bajohn Electrical Conducting Company of St. Louis. This system consisted of metal spikes attached to the top of the stack and connected by copper cables to metal plates buried in the ground 2 feet from the base.

The last phase of this project was completed on July 23 when project supervisor W.H. Goodwin of Brooklyn made the final connections on the installation of a new 500 horsepower generator. The engine was manufactured by C. & G. Cooper of Mount Vernon, Ohio, the company that produced Corliss engines.

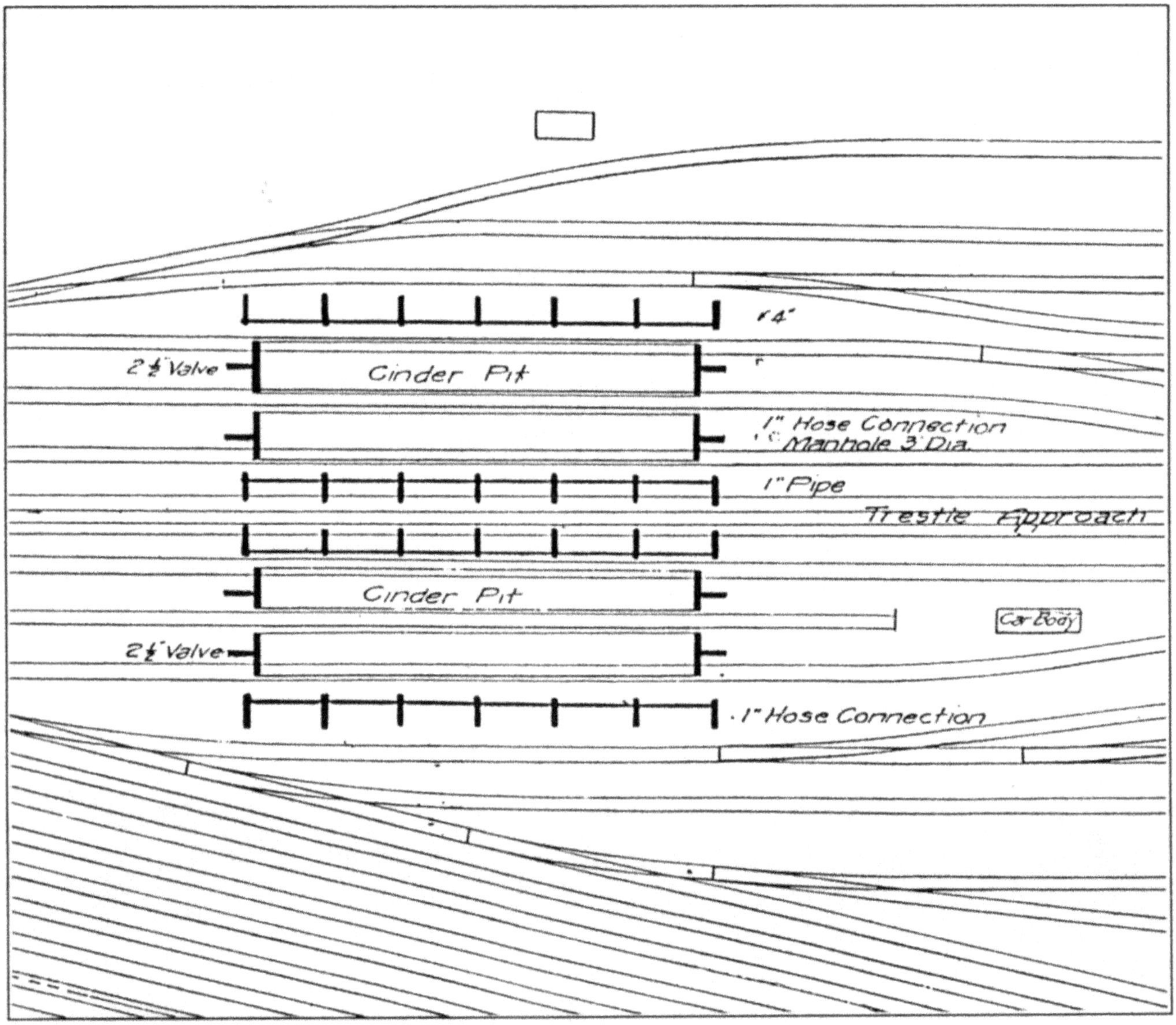

This Company drawing details the new cinder pits that were installed in 1913. (Oneonta City Archives)

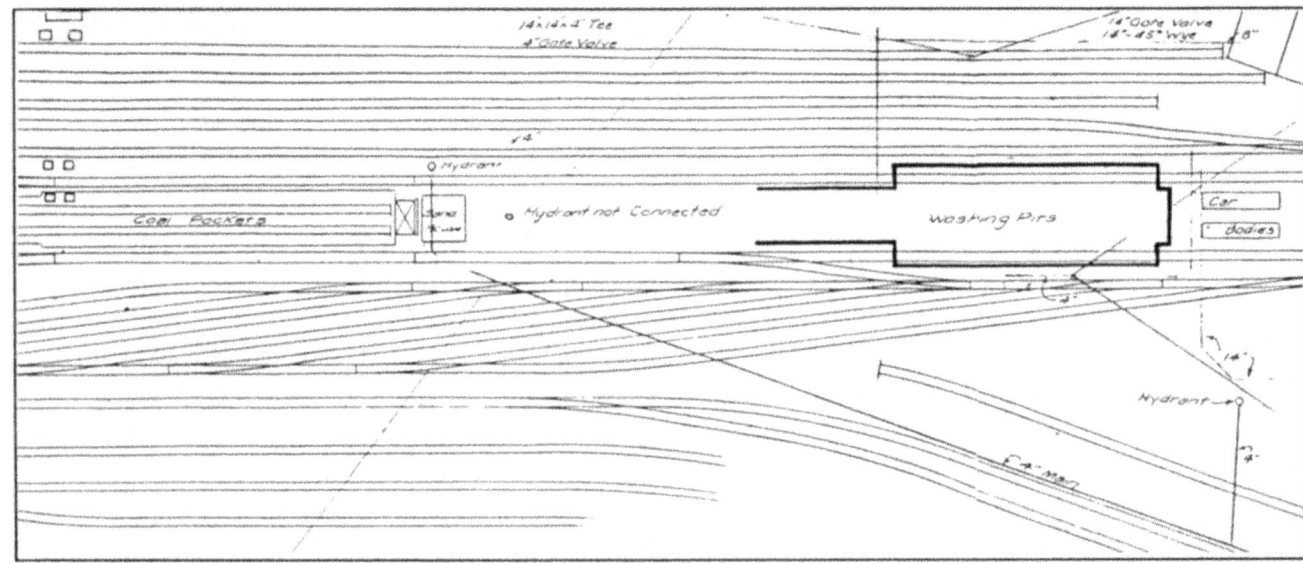

Company drawing showing the original cinder pit after it had been converted to a wash pit. This drawing also shows the car bodies that were assembled for a crew shanty at the head of the pit. (Oneonta City Archives)

This view looking south from the coal pocket shows the two ash pits with their overhead cranes on either side of the trestle. Photographed April 16, 1931. (New York State Library)

The Oneonta Roundhouse, circa 1913. By the time this postcard photo was taken, several changes were evident at the facility. The wood frame blacksmith shop to the right of the building and the smokestack have been completed, and two car bodies have been assembled into a crew shanty at the end of the old cinder pit, which by this time was being used exclusively as a wash pit. (Mrs. Wilmer Bresee)

Obviously leaving open the possibility for future expansion, this generator had the potential to provide five times the demand of the facility at that time.

In 1916 the Delaware and Hudson undertook a major remodeling project at the roundhouse, enlarging the stalls to a sufficient size to accommodate the larger locomotives entering service on the line. The stalls were lengthened 20 feet overall and the Company decided to implement the project in several stages. Work on the first section of seven stalls, numbers 21 through 27, was begun in 1916 and completed in 1917. Seven more stalls, numbers 14 through 20, were completed in 1917-1918. The project was suspended in 1919 during federal control of the railroads and, after work resumed in 1920, 13 more stalls were completed, numbers 1 through 13. This last phase of enlargement was completed in 1921, making a total of 27 stalls that had been upgraded to 100 feet total length.

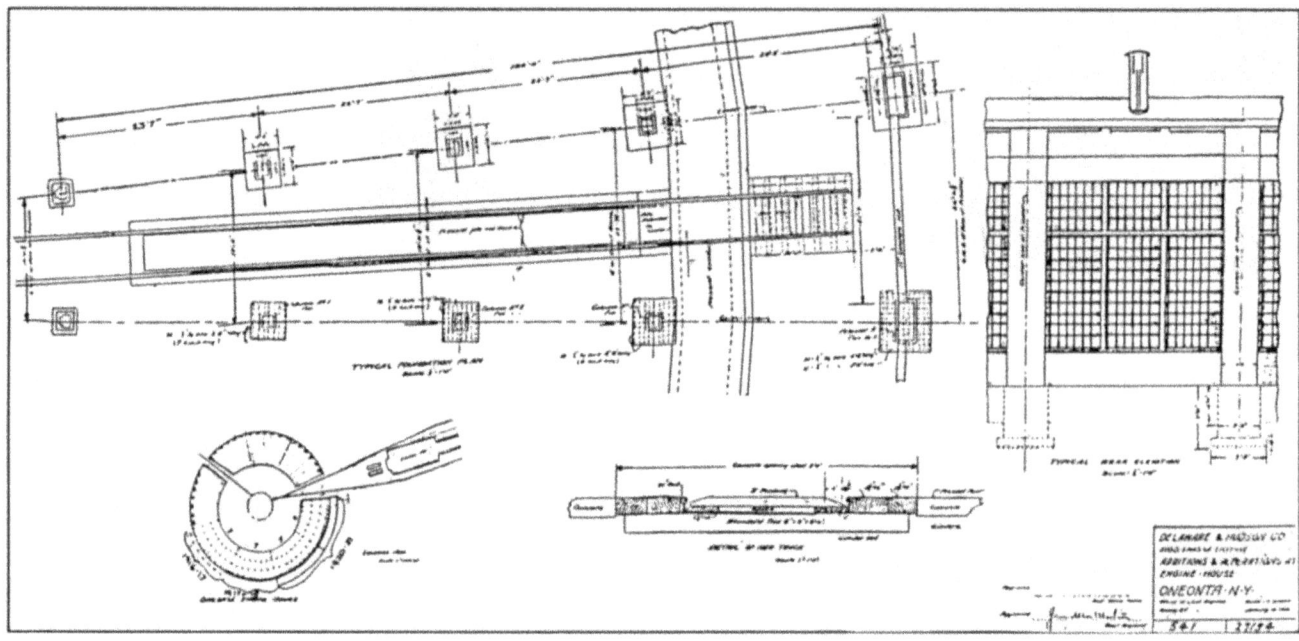

This Company drawing details the series of enlargements made at the Oneonta Roundhouse from 1916 to 1921, and also illustrates the plan of construction. (New York State Historical Association)

Front (left) and rear views taken during the 1921 segment of stall enlargement at the Oneonta Roundhouse. (New York State Historical Association Library)

The remaining 25 stalls were never lengthened due to austerity measures enacted by President Leonor Loree in late 1921. These measures were the result of a serious decline in railroad revenues after World War I, which led the National Railway Board to order mandatory wage cuts for all railway workers in the country.

This move by the government eventually brought about a nationwide strike in 1922 that embroiled Oneonta in a bitter struggle from which the community never completely recovered.

Although the enlargement of the roundhouse stalls was never completed, the Company found that it could not avoid the installation of a longer turntable. This was clearly evident as many of the larger locomotives on the line would not fit on the existing unit without hanging over the ends, thereby making storage and maintenance an impossibility.

The Delaware and Hudson undertook the ambitious project of installing a new 105 foot long turntable on the morning of January 7, 1924. This endeavor was noteworthy in many respects: it was the largest turntable that had ever been installed anywhere in the world; also, it was the first non-balancing unit to be used on the entire system; and, amazingly, the entire project was completed in one day!

The new turntable was manufactured by the Bethlehem Steel Company and was made up of two spans, totaling 105 feet in length. Unique in design, the spans were engineered to distribute the load evenly between the center pivot and circle rail, rather than balancing in the middle, and there were four bearing trucks at the end of each span to carry the load.

The deck spans were joined to a transverse girder at the center and these flexible connections provided for weight deflections and allowed for making adjustments to compensate for errors of elevation between the circle track and center pier. This arrangement also gave the spans freedom to absorb irregularities of level in the circular track in addition to supporting the lateral bracing and intake arch and acting as a jacking beam to release the center casting.

The center pivot consisted of a standard shoe unit comprised of upper shoe, horizontal pin and lower shoe, set on a flat phosphor bronze disc. In addition to the shoe unit, the pivot incorporated many new innovations; it was designed to take the braking force of any engine by means of a phosphor bronze ring around a vertical pin projection of the base casting and the horizontal split pin equalized the load on the disc, transmitting all lateral forces to the lower shoe and through the brake ring to the base casting. The enclosed ring had two wear surfaces, both with provision for self-cleaning and were oil-immersed and oil-trapped, hence able to run in flood waters without damage.

The turntable was designed for efficient maintenance; by actuating the split pin and raising the table less than 1/16", the complete shoe and disc could be removed, inspected and replaced in a fraction of an hour by five men equipped with journal box jacks, wrenches, ropes and gas skids.

The truck frames were cast steel of the "H" type, heavily flanged and braced. Each frame was under-hung from the radially aligned axles of two wheels and supported the girder loads on two radially aligned trunions. This design offered several advantages, including perfect equalization of loads on two wheels of each track and entire freedom of track adjustments for girder level or pivot deflections.

The turntable was powered by two General Electric 35 horsepower motors, arranged so they could be run as a multiple unit or separately. The motors were mounted at either end of the table on platforms, one end of which was suspended from the driven axle, the other end flexibly hung from beams cantilevered from the table.

The load distribution was such that the two driven wheels received 36% of the total weight on track wheels for the unloaded table and 28% for loaded, with any weight engine. The motors were equipped with pinion gear shift and hand power devices for use in case of emergency. The power unit under the operator's cabin was equipped with a foot brake that afforded positive control and it could be connected by drive shaft to a dead engine hauler located on the side of the turntable. The dead engine hauler was operated through gears and a clutch located in the cabin.

The Delaware and Hudson management had made the decision to install a non-balancing turntable because of the many advantages it held over the balancing type: it was less expensive to install and replace, and it was cheaper and easier to maintain due to a simple pin and disc center pivot which was not affected by high water in the pit. Also, during operation the engines did not have to be maneuvered until they were balanced, thus effecting a savings in time, and table rails and approach rails were level at all times thereby eliminating damage to locomotives and track from improper alignment.

Once installed, the new turntable eliminated the frogs in the radial tracks which required a great deal of maintenance. The new table immediately increased the capacity of the facility, being capable of accommodating any locomotive up to 104 feet in length.

Since the Oneonta Terminal was the busiest in the Delaware and Hudson's system, it was imperative that the turntable installation be accomplished in as short a time as possible. Through careful planning and supervision, the entire operation was accomplished in seven hours and thirty-eight minutes, taking the roundhouse out of operation for a total of only ten hours and thirty minutes.

In order to expedite the installation, the work was divided into two segments. First, the preliminary work which consisted of excavation for and construction of the new ring wall and circle track; the supporting of the house tracks between the new ring wall and the old ring wall; the removal of the old ring wall and its replacement with temporary cribbing, and the preparation of the new table to avoid unnecessary work after its installation in the pit. Second, the removal of the old table, cribbing and track carries and installation of the new table.

Work on the project was commenced August 27, 1923, when crews began excavating for the new circle wall. After hand digging proved too slow, a power ditcher was utilized to complete the excavation. Work progressed rapidly, but 5 radial tracks had to be taken out of service at a time. Out of the 5 tracks, however, two were returned to service each night. Therefore, for the 14 hour period, there were only three tracks out of service for at least 12 of the 24 hour period.

As the excavation was being made, timber bents and rail carriers were installed to support the radial tracks and return them to service. The total excavated earth amounted to over 2,000 cubic yards. Excavated material was loaded into air dump cars and hauled by yard switchers, to a dump track at the edge of the swamp. Some difficulty was experienced in the excavation due to the fact that the ground at this location consisted of fill resting on an old swamp, resulting in about two feet of water being encountered while the work was being done. Steam siphons and a centrifugal pump were used to remove water from the pit, thereby avoiding any major work interruptions.

Immediately following excavation, concrete footing was poured and scrap pieces of boiler flue were set to act as supports for the new circle rail. Once this had been accomplished the circle wall was poured, with the circle rail anchors being firmly embedded in the cement. Once the circle wall had cured sufficiently, the back wall was poured, thereby completing the new circle. A concrete mixer mounted on flanged trucks was used throughout the pouring of walls.

The removal of the old concrete circle was begun on November 21. Initially the work was done with jackhammers, but this proved to be too time consuming so dynamite was used to break up the remainder. Removal of the old walls was completed on December 12 and cribbing was installed to temporarily support the tracks. At this point it was necessary to install new timbers between the new back wall and the new circle wall in order to carry the radial tracks, and this work was completed on January 2nd.

Due to the design differences in the non-balancing table, a higher center pivot was required for the new unit. In order to avoid a delay in construction, a precast center block was made on October 26 and allowed to cure thoroughly before installation. A precast counterweight was also poured, which was later installed at the end of the new table, diametrically opposed to the control cabin.

At this point the pit was ready to receive the new turntable, the only work remaining being the cutting of the radial tracks to the new length and the removal of cribbing and temporary rail carries. The new turntable was delivered on December 20 and the ties for the deck were framed while the concrete for the new pit was being poured.

Once the pit was ready, a meeting was held in the Division Engineer's office to plan the strategy for installing the table and placing it in operation in the least amount of time possible. Once the table had been unloaded, the steel gang made all the connections that were possible prior to installation, then the trucks were placed in position and blocked in the pit, allowing the new table to sit directly upon the truck mountings. Most of the setup work was done prior to installation, including placement of deck ties, conduits, wiring for motors, gallows frame for the power connector at the center, cabin controls and number 1 motor. The power lines to the collector had been run prior to the installation and the two 4 foot long sections between the two halves of the table were precut and fitted with unions, enabling the final connections to be made in less than an hour.

Before the day of installation, a bridge erecting crane and a locomotive erecting crane were brought to the site and used to determine the balance point on each half of the new table, which was marked so as to save time during installation.

On the night of January 6, all engines were turned and all locomotives that would be needed for the following day were removed. Radial tracks were also cut at the new ring wall during the night. All the necessary equipment including cranes, flat cars and gondolas were placed on the appropriate radial tracks by 8:00 AM, January 7. Power was shut off at 8:07 and crews immediately began the removal of rail, cribbing and ties from the old table.

Once the cribbing was removed, crews moved swiftly; at 9:40 a.m. the old table was lifted out, loaded onto flat cars and backed into the roundhouse. Immediately thereafter, the bridge erecting crane removed the old center bearing and the foundation was cleaned and mortar mixed with plaster of paris was applied to bind the new center block. The new precast block was set in place at 10:50 a.m. and the new center bearing was set in place at 11:17 a.m. The first half of the new table was set in place at 12:00 p.m. and the second half followed at 12:20 p.m.. The bolting up of the two spans was started at 12:41 p.m. and completed at 3:30 p.m. The electrical work was started at noon and motor number 1 was ready for service at 1:20 p.m..

At 3:05 p.m., all electrical work was completed and both motors were ready for service. The placement of rails and the tie plates on the new deck was started at 12:20 p.m. and completed at 2:30 p.m..

Once the gallows frame had been secured, linemen made the connection at the power collector, which was designed so that the table could revolve independently of the power connection.

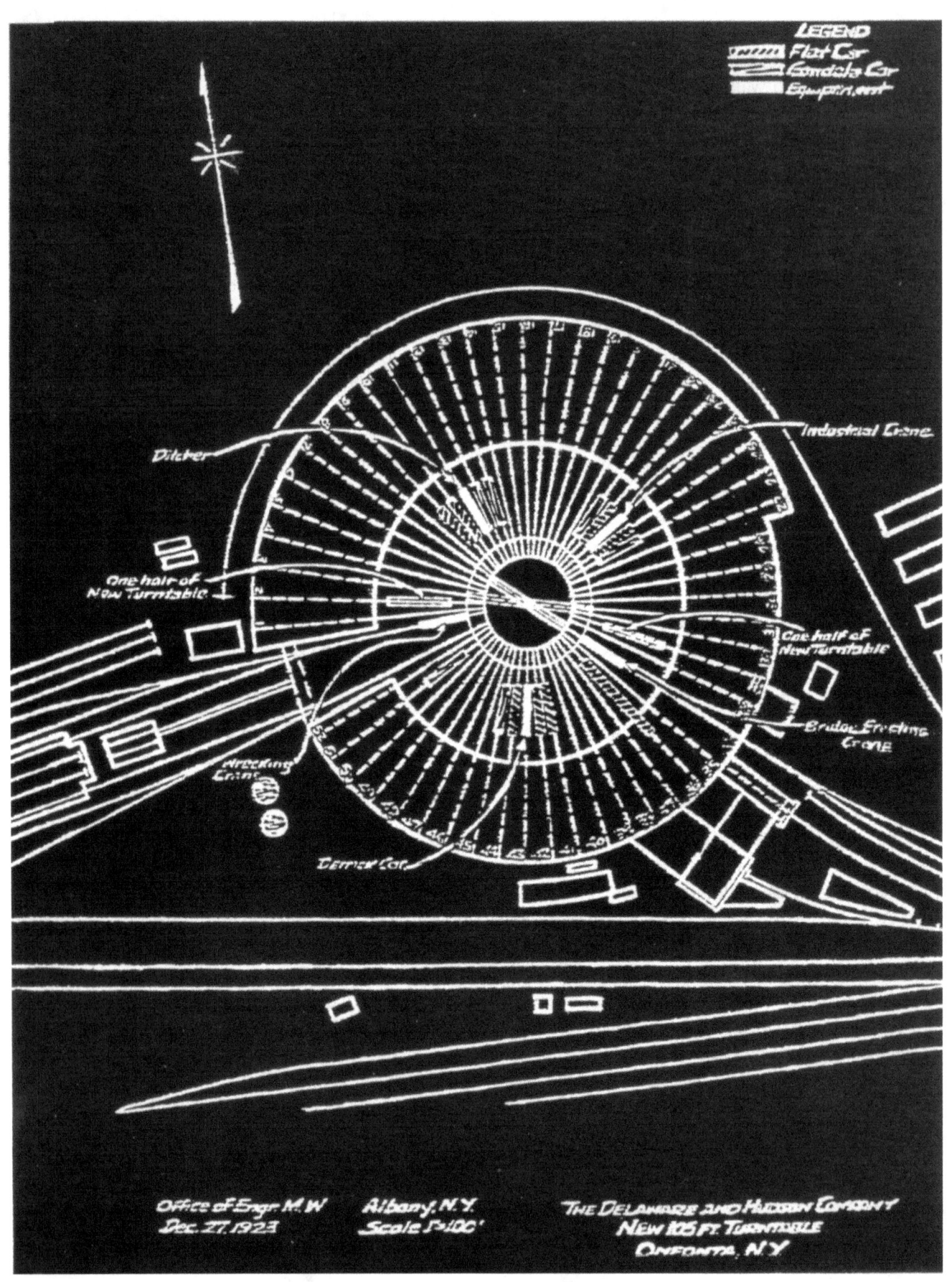

D. & H. Company drawing showing the operational setup for the installation of the new 105 foot turntable on January 27, 1924. (LRHS Collection)

9:00 a.m., 1/7/24: Taking out blocking in preparation for removal of old turntable. (LRHS Collection)

While the final electrical connections were being made, crews were removing the balance of the rails, concrete and cribbing. At 3:30 p.m., the entire project had been completed and at 3:45 the new turntable made its first revolution and was turned over to the Mechanical Department for operation. The total time consumed from the shutting off of power to the first revolution was 7 hours and 38 minutes, an exceptional time for a project of this magnitude.

Once the new turntable was in operation, Oneonta could claim the dual distinction of possessing the largest turntable in the world, operating in the largest roundhouse in the world.

9:10 a.m., 1/7/24: Old turntable being prepared for removal. (LRHS Collection)

9:40 a.m., 1/7/24: Raising old turntable from pit. (LRHS Collection)

9:45 a.m., 1/7/24: Swinging old turntable clear of pit. (LRHS Collection)

10:50 a.m., 1/7/24: Setting precast center block while old table is loaded on cars. (LRHS Collection)

12:00 noon, 1/7/24: Placing south half of of new table in pit. (LRHS Collection)

12:20 p.m., 1/7/24: Placing north half of turntable in pit. (LRHS Collection)

1:00 p.m., 1/7/24: New turntable in place. (LRHS Collection)

1:30 p.m., 1/7/24: Longitudinal view of new turntable in place. (LRHS Collection)

Left - 3/4 view of new table showing dead engine hauler. (LRHS Collection)

Right - 3/4 view showing catenary supporting power cables. (LRHS Collection)

Left - 3/4 view of table showing "H" fixture and cable supports. (LRHS Collection)

Right - Power transformer and main switch box. (LRHS Collection)

Left - Central power control cabinet. (LRHS Collection)

Right - Transformers and power line. (LRHS Collection)

A major addition to the Oneonta roundhouse was initiated in the fall of 1926 when D. & H. General Manager J. T. Loree announced the construction of a new machine shop to replace the old facility located in the "back shop." The new building was to be directly attached to the roundhouse and the project included the removal of two stall end walls to allow for a direct connection between the buildings.

The contract for construction was awarded to Austin and Company of New York City, and work was commenced immediately. On October 13, the wood frame office building of Master Mechanic George Brown was moved south from the roundhouse and the construction site was leveled and graded. The Company's goal was to complete the structure as quickly as possible, so crews pushed their work through the winter months, with the structure being completed and put into use in February of 1927.

This photo of the turntable intake arch was taken on June 4, 1925, the year after the new 105 foot turntable was installed. (New York State Library)

The new machine shop was a significant addition to the Delaware and Hudson facilities at Oneonta. The building measured 130 feet by 230 feet and was of steel construction with brick and concrete walls. The first floor contained all the latest machinery available for use in repairing and fabricating locomotive components, and the second floor housed the Master Mechanic's office, in addition to space for the dispatcher, clerks and bookkeepers. The total cost of construction was over $200,000.00, and an additional $25,000.00 was invested in machinery, which the company felt to be a worthwhile expenditure in view of the savings that would be realized by having the roundhouse and machine shop directly connected.

The improvements included the installation of a Whiting electric hoist which was capable of lifting the locomotives as high as seven feet off the ground. With a capacity of 200 tons, this hoist greatly expedited the changing of locomotive wheels on any of the Company's power units. The new equipment also included a traveling electric crane which was used for moving heavy components such as boiler fronts, crossheads, connecting rods and stacks. The crane had an adjustable boom, making it very maneuverable in tight spaces.

A monorail electric hoist system connected the roundhouse with all sections of the machine shop and it incorporated electric switches so that heavy pieces of machinery could be transported to any location for repair.

The blacksmith shop housed three forges, each equipped with forced draft and suction exhaust to prevent gases from escaping into the building. A large oil furnace was used for melting brass and babbitt for bushings, and oil heat was also used in the large annealing furnace where pins and other components were case hardened by baking in Imperlite for 16 hours. The blacksmith shop also housed the Electrical Department, responsible for the maintenance and repair of lighting, generating and train control equipment. In addition, a section of the building was used for the rod shop which was equipped with a hydraulic press for fitting new bushings and an Ohio shaper for planing bearings and crosshead bushings.

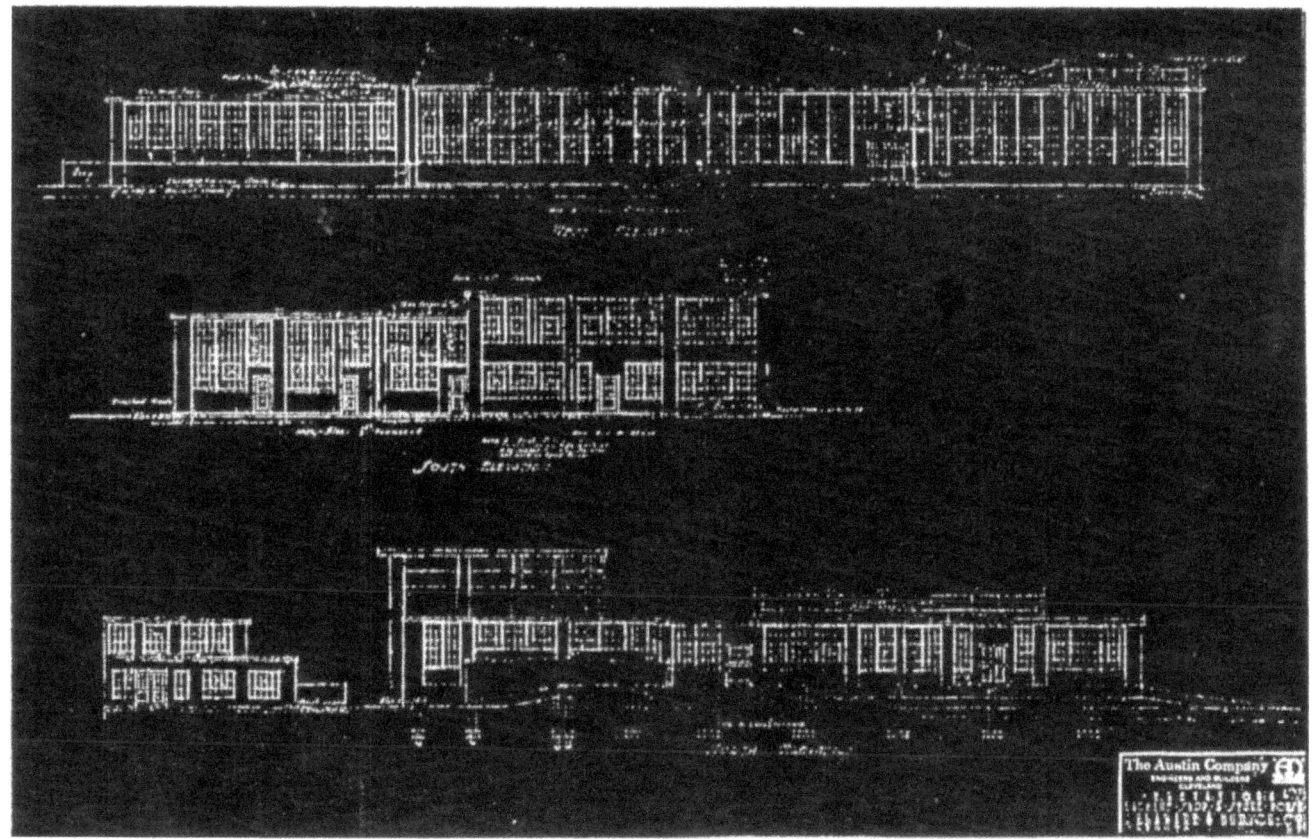

Architect's drawing of the new machine shop at Oneonta, opened in 1927. (LRHS Collection)

This outstanding shot of the Whiting electric hoist in operation was taken on April 16, 1937. (New York State Library)

The new machine shop building incorporated an expansive storeroom which was designed to make parts and supplies easily accessible. A washrack, which consisted of a hot bath heated by steam coils, was located outside the storeroom.

In addition to office space, the new building contained a storage area for shovels and drinking pails. The owner's name was on each pail and the pails were arranged alphabetically. The building also housed an up-to-date first aid room, well equipped to handle any minor injuries.

In the summer of 1927 the old machine shop was converted into an employee locker room which was kept locked except at meal hours and changes of shift. The Company devised a very innovative system, in which each employee was given a number which corresponded with a bucket on an endless chain, and the individual worker would raise his belongings to the ceiling and lock the chain with a padlock, thereby securing his possessions and also avoiding congestion on the floor. This system also provided a means of drying clothing during wet weather. Shortly after completion of the locker room, an employee bathroom with shower was installed in addition to a reading room on the second floor.

The interior of the new machine shop as it appeared on April 16, 1931, with a spotless floor and not a tool out of place. The track in the foreground was used to move wheels from the roundhouse into the shop. (New York State Library)

Once the new machine shop had been put into service, the D. & H. embarked on a major restructuring of the Oneonta Yards under the direction of Divisional Foreman A. G. Ditmore. The Company's objective was to increase the volume of repairs done at the shops without adding manpower, and this was accomplished by streamlining the facility.

The first step in the reorganization was the combining of building 7, the old "back shop," with building 8 which housed the coach shop. The two departments were actually in the same building but fire walls were taken out to form one large repair shop fed by three incoming tracks.

In order to expedite car repairs, the lumber yard and paint shop were relocated to a site nearer the repair shop and all unnecessary structures, including the original roundhouses and turntables, were dismantled. Also, scales were installed adjacent to the repair shop to eliminate the time involved in hauling cars to the hump to be weighed.

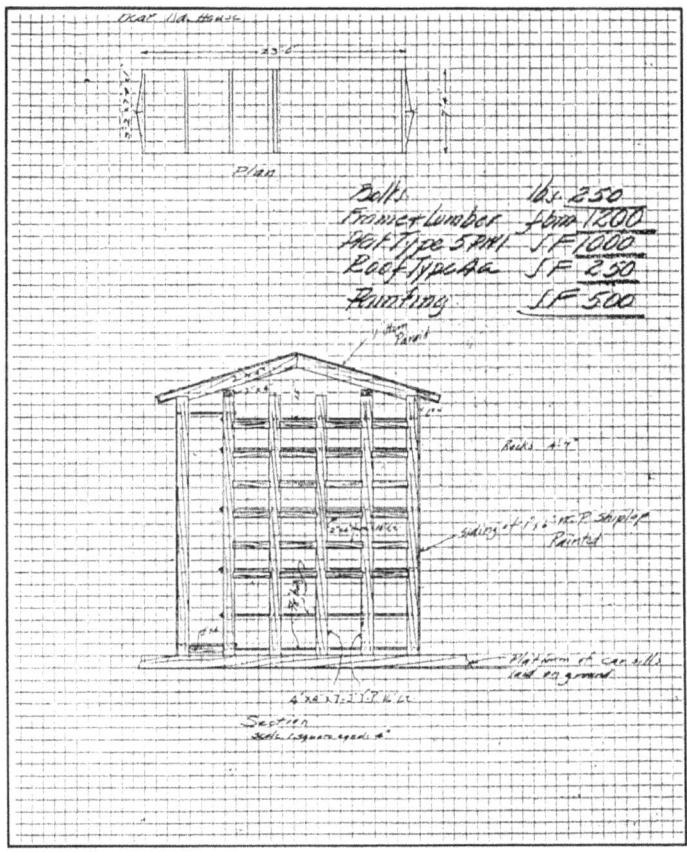

As part of the reconstruction project, the power house was updated and had automatic stokers installed which made possible the burning of smaller, more efficient birds-eye coal. Also at this time, the company overhauled a large tank for washing locomotive water. Water from locomotives was pumped into this tank where it was kept hot and where impurities were removed so that engines ready for use could be filled with water already at 200 degrees, thereby cutting down on start up time.

Pipe rack adjacent to storeroom. (National Records Center, Washington, D.C.)

Two views of the oil storage tanks, which were located in the basement of the storeroom. Photographed April 18, 1931. (New York State Library)

This photo shows the oil distribution pumps, which were fed by pipelines from tanks in the basement. Photographed April 16, 1931. (New York State Library)

Interior of employee locker room, showing the unique arrangement of pails on endless chains. The workers were able to keep their lunches secure by locking the pail in place at the ceiling. Photographed April 16, 1931. (New York State Library)

These two views, both taken from the coal trestle, show the Oneonta Roundhouse before and after the new machine shop was annexed to the building. The one on the left was taken on June 4, 1925; the one on the right was taken April 16, 1931. (New York State Library)

Interior of heating plant showing boilers and automatic stoker. Photographed April 16, 1931. (New York State Library)

This rare photograph of a Dickenson smoke jack in use was taken on March 16, 1931. (New York State Library)

This magnificent array of motive power was photographed on April 16, 1931. Note the meticulous condition of the building, which was standard procedure during the days of steam on the D. & H. (New York State Library)

This view of the turntable and a fully occupied roundhouse was photographed April 16, 1931. (New York State Library)

Two youngsters posed on the pilot of #1122 in their Sunday best makes for a beautiful composition in this photo taken April 16, 1931. The awnings on the machine shop windows were typical of the aesthetic touches found throughout Oneonta Yards during the golden years of the D. & H., when a proper Sunday stroll would include a tour of the flower gardens maintained by the shop crews. (New York State Library)

These two views from Table Rocks, taken 20 years apart, graphically illustrate the improvements made to the Oneonta Roundhouse during that time period. The photo on the left was taken about 1908. At this time the only new construction at the facility was the installation of a pump house on the Susquehanna River and a water main running from there to the building. The right hand photo, taken in 1928, shows the 160 foot smokestack that was added to the power plant in 1913, and the new machine shop that was constructed in 1927. Also the section of the building in the foreground, stalls number 1 through 27, were lengthened by 20 feet in the years 1916 through 1921, and a new 105 foot turntable was installed in 1924. (Author"s Collection)

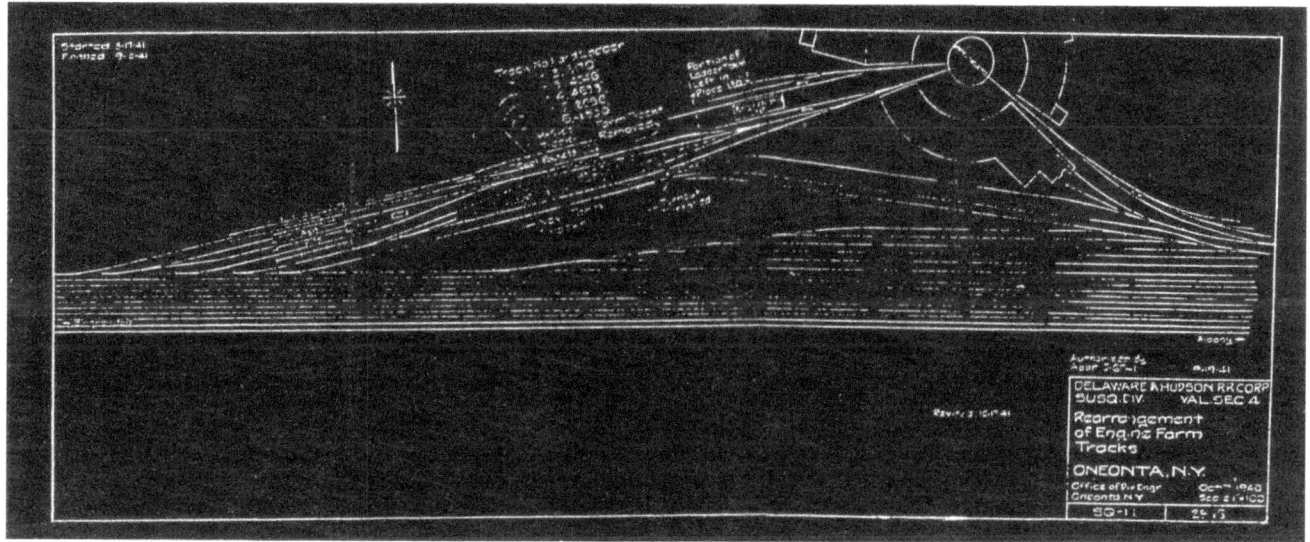

This Company drawing dated September 1941 details the rearrangement of engine farm tracks at the Oneonta Engine facility, and shows the location of the cinder pits that were installed in 1913. (LRHS Collection)

This aerial photograph of the Oneonta Roundhouse was taken in the late 1940's, and provides a composite history of the building's evolution between 1906 and 1944. The section in the foreground, comprised of stalls number 35 through 52, has not been modified and represents the original plan of construction, including the vintage skylights with windows on both sides. The only visible improvement in this section is the 160 foot smokestack that was erected in 1913. Directly across the incoming tracks, moving clockwise around the building, is the first enlargement of 20 feet which was added between 1916 and 1921, involving stalls 1 through 27. To the extreme left of the building is the second machine shop, which was built in 1927. Once again moving clockwise, halfway around the rear section of the building can be seen the final enlargement which was made in 1942 and 1944, and included stalls 15 through 33. Note the progressive movement of the smoke jacks toward the outside of the building, as the motive units continued to grow in length. In the middle of the roundhouse circle is the 105 foot turntable that was installed in 1924. (LRHS Collection)

CHAPTER FOUR

THE CHALLENGERS

The last major enlargements to be made at the Oneonta Roundhouse took place in 1942 and 1944, changes that were made necessary by the introduction of Challenger locomotives onto the line in June of 1940. In February of that year, a delegation of D. & H. officials toured the building in anticipation of modifications that would be required in order to accommodate the massive power units. Officials later announced the purchase of 20 class 4-6-6-4 Mallet locomotives, at a cost of $178,900.00 each. The huge locomotives required modifications on many of the Company's bridges and turntables, although no changes were made on the Oneonta turntable. It was necessary, however, to lengthen stalls 15 through 33 at the Oneonta roundhouse to accommodate the new engines which were 116 feet long, including tender. This project was implemented in two stages: the first six stalls, numbers 28 through 33, were lengthened 51 feet in January of 1942, and thirteen more stalls, numbers 15 through 27, were lengthened 31 feet in July of 1944. The second phase of expansion required an extension of only 31 feet, as stalls 15 through 27 had already been extended by 20 feet in 1916-1918. Unlike the earlier enlargement which matched the brick and concrete of the original building, the Challenger addition utilized wood frame construction, obviously a cost-cutting measure. Although the 105 foot turntable could handle the locomotive by itself, it was necessary to move the tender across separately with a switcher or dead engine puller.

The decision to purchase the Challengers had been made by D.&H. President Joseph H. Nuelle, who took over the Company in 1938. At that time the railroad industry was in state of transition, with a great deal of freight transportation being taken over by other modes of transportation. In addition, the demand for coal, the Company's mainstay, had declined as other forms of fuel gained popularity.

In order to compensate for the decreased demand for coal, the new President focused his attention on increasing the amount of "bridge traffic" between New England and Canada. To do this, the Company would have to haul more coal in less time and President Nuelle decided that the best means to this end would be through the purchase of more powerful motive units. Therefore, the order was placed with Alco for 20 of the Challenger locomotives, to be delivered in 1940.

The original Challenger locomotive was conceived by Otto Jabelmann of the Union Pacific and the first unit was built by Alco in 1936. Among the articulateds, the Challengers were outstanding for their speed and agility. Their design allowed for excellent balance and the 4-6-6-4's built after 1939 had enough weight on the front end to reduce the slippage that was common to earlier articulateds.

All Challengers had either 69" or 70" drivers and tractive effort ranged from 94,400 pounds on the Delaware and Hudson to 106,900 pounds on the Northern Pacific. The 4-6-6-4 was a dual purpose engine and often saw duty in passenger service, but its main task was heavy, fast freight. Speeds up to 70 miles per hour were safe because of the excellent balancing of the side rods, especially on the later models.

The original Challengers had 22" X 32" cylinders, 69" drivers, 255 pounds steam pressure, weighed 556,000 pounds and were rated at 97,400 pounds tractive effort. The units built for the Delaware and Hudson were rated at 285 pounds of pressure with 20 1/2" cylinders.

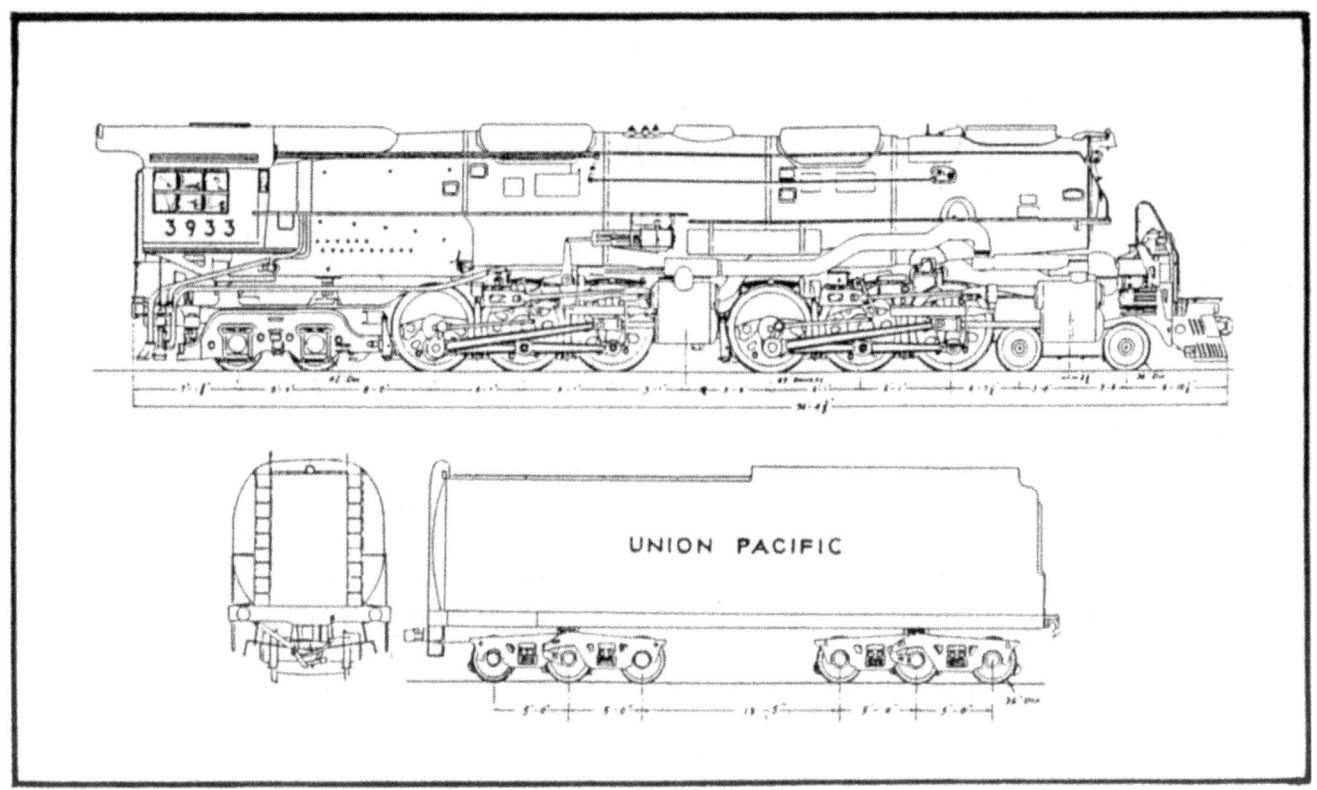

Schematic of Union Pacific Challenger, similar in many respects to the Delaware and Hudson units. (Power Plan for the Union Pacific Railroad)

The first D.&H. Challenger, number 1500, steamed out of the Alco shops on June 24, 1940 and was inspected by Company General Manager Glenn H. Caley. It was soon followed by numbers 1501 through 1519. The Challenger purchase was considered to be such a milestone event that the management announced plans to take the locomotives on a tour of the system, making stops at stations along the line to allow spectators the chance to preview the new engines.

The first D. & H. Challenger, Number 1500, delivered June 24, 1940. (New York State Library)

On July 4th and 5th, 1940, Challenger #1503 was placed on display in Oneonta and the massive machine proved to be a major attraction for the city. An estimated 10,000 people toured the locomotive during the two day period, many traveling from the far reaches of Otsego and Delaware counties. Special platforms and steps were erected to allow access to the cab and lights were strung the length of the engine to provide night time illumination. Company guides were on hand to point out the mechanical aspects of the engine and also answer any questions put forth by the visitors. All who toured the new locomotive were awed by its sheer size and power.

Challenger #1500, Oneonta, New York, Late 1940's. (Trackside Photos/LRHS Collection)

Challenger # 1501 on display at Albany, New York, summer 1940. (New York State Library/LRHS Collection)

Builder's photograph of Challenger #1505. (Tim Truscott)

Delaware & Hudson publicity photograph of Challenger #1505. This unit was actually built in 1940, not 1945 as shown in the nomenclature. (Author's collection)

Challenger #1509, Oneonta, New York, late 1940's. (Trackside Photos/LRHS Collection)

The Challenger's specifications were indeed impressive. The overall length of the unit was 116 feet, 8 1/2 inches, including tender. The total weight, with tender, was 986,000 pounds with 205,500 pounds on the drivers alone. The engine was equipped with automatic coal stokers, and could easily do 65 miles per hour. The tractive power was 95,000 pounds, 40 percent more than the 2-8-0's in use at the time. The firebox surface totaled 633 square feet and the tender capacity was 22,500 gallons of water and 26 tons of coal. The engine was also designed with the comfort and safety of the crew in mind, as the cab incorporated upholstered seats, clothes lockers, a screened ventilator and shatterproof glass.

The Challenger locomotives were so successful that the Company purchased another 15 units, numbers 1520-1534, in 1942. Due to the wartime economy, the price had increased to $213,500.00 each. A final purchase of 5 units, numbers 1535-1539, was made in 1946. This would be the last purchase of steam locomotives made by the Delaware and Hudson, as the Company had already begun to dieselize by the mid-1940's.

All the Company's Challenger locomotives were scrapped between 1952 and 1953.

Challenger #1513, Oneonta, New York, late 1940's. (Trackside Photos/LRHS Collection)

Challenger #1514, Oneonta, New York, late 1940's. (Trackside Photos/LRHS Collection)

Challenger #1515 under steam. (Power Plan for the Union Pacific Railroad)

Challenger #1517, Oneonta, New York, late 1940's. (Trackside Photos/LRHS Collection)

Challenger #1531 waiting to be scrapped, Carbondale, Pennsylvania; September 4, 1952. (Author's collection)

Challenger #1537, date and location unknown. (Trackside Photos/Jim Gale)

Challenger #1537, early 1950's, location unknown. (Author's collection)

Challenger #1537 at Delanson Station, August 8, 1950. (Author's collection)

Challenger #1539, Oneonta, New York, late 1940's. (Trackside Photos/LRHS Collection)

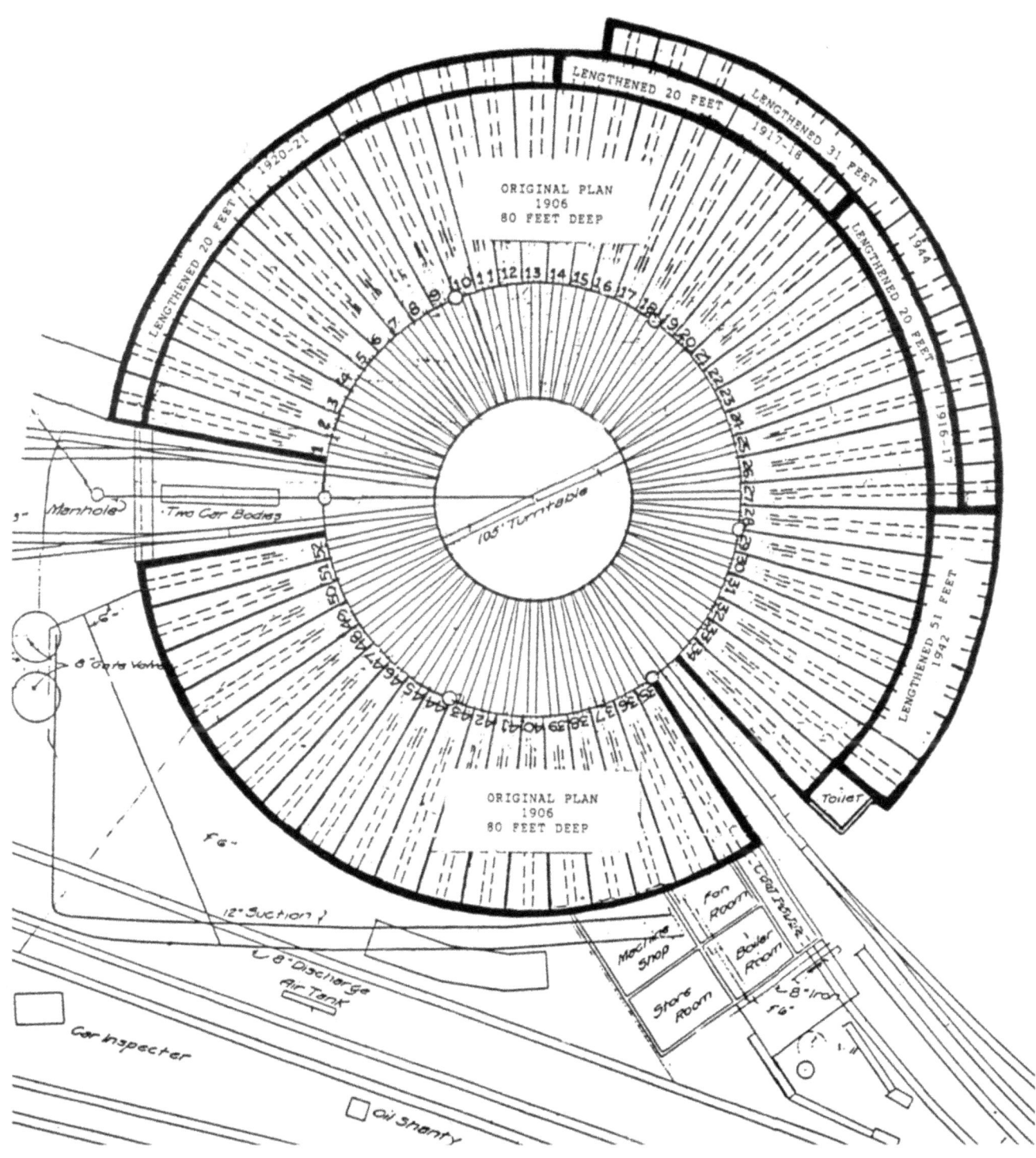

The drawing above details the chronology of enlargements at the Oneonta Roundhouse from 1916 through 1944. (Oneonta City Archives)

CHAPTER FIVE

THE COAL POCKET FIRE

On the morning of March 13, 1946, the Oneonta Engine Terminal suffered the worst tragedy in its history. At 11:23 a.m. that morning, the Oneonta Fire Department responded to an alarm at the Oneonta Roundhouse. Upon arriving, they found the coal pocket fully engulfed in flames, with eight loaded coal cars and two loaded sand cars sitting on the track above the chutes. Each one of the coal cars was filled to capacity, bearing 50 tons of coal. Four hoses were laid immediately and connected to the facility hydrants but the water pressure in the Company mains proved inadequate to effectively fight the blaze. To make matters worse, a strong wind began fanning the fire, which was already being propelled by the creosote-covered beams and joists.

The fire had been started by a worker using an acetylene torch to burn metal in one of the bins at the center of the chute and, once ignited, flames immediately began to shoot high into the air.

As the fire raged out of control, police and firemen warned spectators, numbering about 500, to withdraw from the immediate area as a precaution against the possible collapse of the structure and the cars on the top. The roaring flames were punctuated from time to time by explosions from bursting air and gas containers.

Due to the lack of sufficient water pressure, it was impossible for the firemen to contain the flames and soon sparks had started a grass fire at Table Rocks. After dispatching a crew to deal with this blaze, another fire was ignited at one of the water towers near the roundhouse. After the firefighters succeeded in quelling this blaze, another one ignited in the roundhouse roof, so the entire roof area was soaked. This proved to be an extremely difficult task due to the meager water supply. With the Oneonta Fire Department so heavily involved in fighting widespread fires, Fire Chief Michael Stapleton called in the Otego squad to man the Oneonta station in the event of any further emergencies.

As the fire was progressing rapidly, the D. & H. foreman at the site made a fateful decision. Twelve men were sent to the top of the trestle with acetylene torches, with orders to separate the burning coal chute from the trestle, so as to save as much of the structure as possible. The foreman's plan was to have the workers cut the rails and steel work a safe distance from the flames, thereby creating a firebreak.

By 1:00 p.m., the crew had succeeded in cutting through the rails and partially separating the trestle from the coal chute. By this time the heat from the flames had grown so intense that the firefighters were forced to withdraw from the scene. In spite of the severity of the situation, the workers continued cutting, unaware that most of the timbers had burned away, leaving the ten loaded cars sitting on nothing but rails.

Suddenly at 1:10 p.m., the structure began to collapse. At this point the flames were within 30 feet of the workers and, realizing the immediate danger, they attempted to scramble for safety. But it was too late. Beginning at the sand pocket end, within 60 seconds the momentum of the falling structure had reached the point where the men were engaged in their task. The crew members were hurled into the air, appearing to onlookers as a human shower falling to the ground.

As rescue workers risked their own lives to reach the victims, they found that the coal chute collapse had taken a tragic toll in life and limb; eleven people had been injured, one fatally. A second worker would die from injuries the following day. The accident casualties were:

- Claude Simmons, 43, West Oneonta, fractured skull, died of injuries March 13, 1946.
- James Lindberg, 39, 18 Park Avenue, Oneonta, fractured skull, died of injuries March 14, 1946.
- Howard Sands, 31, 13 Columbia Street, Oneonta, fractured back.
- Harry Palmer, 46, 12 Forest Avenue, Oneonta, fractured back.
- Clayton Loucks, 43, 46 Oneida Street, Oneonta, chest injury.
- Claude Dexter, 34, Davenport Center, injuries to ankle and arm.
- Harold Barney, 28, West Oneonta, fractured left arm and compound fracture of left ankle.
- Henry Christiansen, 40, Nineveh Junction, chest injury, lacerations and bruises.
- Francis Riley, 34, 3 Huntington Avenue, Oneonta, back injury.
- Donald Phillips, 20, Otego, right hip injury.
- Clinton Alger, 37, Otego, lacerations.

James Lindberg of Oneonta was one of the two men who lost their lives in the coal pocket fire. (LRHS Collection)

Miraculously, the 12th man on the trestle escaped the collapse while running an errand. Keith Wier, 43, of East Street, Oneonta, had been ordered by the foreman to get the lunch pails for the men working on the trestle. Mr. Wier reached the ground only moments before the structure collapsed. Three Oneonta policemen also narrowly escaped injury; Chief Robert Simmons, Sargent Frank Golding and Officer Rivera were leading one of the victims to a squad car when another section of the structure gave way, sending the men diving into a pile of coal as debris flew over their heads.

After the collapse, spectators, police and firemen did their best to aid the injured workers. Three ambulances were pressed into service shuttling the victims to the hospital where D. & H. surgeon Dr. Alexander Carson was assisted by Dr. Cornelius Ryan and Dr. Norman Getman in handling the emergency.

Fed by the 400 tons of coal that had been in the 8 gondolas, the fire burned on for several days, hampering efforts to remove the toppled cars from the wreckage. The heat had been so intense that the sand in the cars had melted to glass.

Shortly after the fire an investigation was conducted into the possible causes of the tragedy, focusing on the foreman's decision to send the men up on the burning trestle. It was eventually decided that there had been no way of anticipating the collapse of the trestle section where the men were working and that they had not deliberately been put in jeopardy.

The Company also investigated the problem of low water pressure which had made battling the blaze so difficult and found that the arm on a shaft controlling the fire pump was broken. The arm and an attached magnet controlled the pilot valve on the altitude valve when the pump was in service and, if the mechanism was not operating properly, it made the pump inoperable. Interestingly, a fire drill had been conducted the previous day, at which time the pump was operating perfectly. The D. & H. could offer no explanation for the system's sudden malfunction.

The Company estimated its loss in the coal pocket fire at $150,000.00, as $50,000.00 had been invested the previous year in upgrading the structure. Until a replacement structure could be built, sanding was done by derricks and coaling was done by the ash pit cranes.

Remains of the coal trestle after the fire.

After the coal pocket fire, locomotives were temporarily coaled by the ash pit cranes until a new coaling station could be constructed.

In June of 1946 the Delaware and Hudson began construction on a huge coal tower to replace the coal chute that had been lost in the fire. The contract for erecting the structure was awarded to the Roberts and Schaefer Company of Chicago and work was commenced with a force of 75 men under the direction of superintendent Jack Clark.

In order to support the weight of the tower, hardwood piles were driven 80 feet into the swampy ground. A makeshift pile driver had been assembled from a "stiff-legged" derrick mounted on a moveable base resting on large rollers. The machine was fitted with a pile hammer that delivered a 25 ton blow, fed by steam from a nearby locomotive.

While excavating for the coal pit, workers unearthed two subterranean streams which were fed by the Susquehanna River. Four pumps were kept in operation constantly to remove water from these streams while the foundation was being poured.

Work on the tower continued through the summer and into fall, with the new coaling facility being put into use in December of 1946. Construction was entirely of steel reinforced concrete, and the total height of the tower was over 100 feet. Instead of the previous system of running up a trestle to dump their coal into bins, the new coaling plant incorporated a cement lined hopper on the ground which received the contents of incoming coal cars. The coal would then be transferred by electric conveyor to a receiving hopper at the top of the tower, and from there went into a revolving hopper that deposited the coal into three pockets, with a combined capacity of 450 tons. From the pockets the coal passed through 8 outlets that fed directly into the locomotive tenders. The tower had a loading capacity of 100 tons per hour and could load 4 locomotives with coal in that time period.

A new sanding plant was also built adjacent to the coal tower, which incorporated 2 small towers, each one feeding into 4 outlets. The two towers provided a combined capacity of 100 tons and could load and unload their capacity several times daily.

The new coaling facility was completed at a total cost of over $250,000.00 and would be the last addition made at the Oneonta Engine Terminal.

Four views of the combination coaling and sanding plant that was installed in the summer of 1946.

Note: All photographs in this chapter, with the exception of James Lindberg (p. 73), are from the New York State Library.

CHAPTER SIX

THE END OF AN ERA

In 1954, Oneonta witnessed the sad demise of the mammoth structure that had dominated the landscape of west end for nearly half a century. On July 11, the Delaware and Hudson Railroad announced that the roundhouse was being closed, effective immediately. The Company also disclosed that seven sand drying facilities throughout the system would be shut down and consolidated at Oneonta.

On December 2, 1954, the Schesser Demolition Company of Scranton, Pennsylvania began the somber task of dismantling the landmark structure, with the project claiming 36 of the 52 stalls, leaving only a small remnant of its past glory remaining. Of the 16 stalls left standing, 3 were occupied by the D. & H. Bridge and Building Department and the balance were leased to Enterprise Aluminum Company on River Street, with the last tenant being Agrico Fertilizer.

This view of the Oneonta Roundhouse was taken from Franklin Mountain in 1954, shortly before the building was dismantled. Part of the first smokestack has already been taken down, and 36 of the building's stalls will be claimed by the wrecking ball before the project is completed. (Tom Oliver / Carmen Vagliardo)

As the building was being demolished, many old-timers watched sadly as the giant structure was brought down. Among them were George and Clifford Sullivan, both of whom had worked on the 1921 enlargement. Neither of the Sullivans thought they would ever see the day when the roundhouse would be gone. Also witnessing the demolition was Foreman H. M. Loucks, who reminisced about the growth in locomotive size over the years of his tenure, through 900's, 100's, 1200's and finally the 1500-class behemoths.

In order to drastically cut overhead costs, the Delaware and Hudson embarked on similar demolition projects at Colonie, Saratoga Springs, Whitehall and Mechanicville. The Oneonta segment of the project also called for the demolition of two smokestacks and the removal of an auxiliary track from Gas Avenue east to Colliersville.

Further cost-cutting measures included the removal of storage tracks at Nineveh and passing tracks at Bainbridge, Sidney and Worcester. In addition, turntables at Cherry Valley, Cooperstown and Oneonta were cut up and scrapped.

This unfortunate chapter in Oneonta's railroad history was brought about by the Company's rapid conversion to diesel power after World War 2, with steam power being completely eliminated by 1952. Between 1952 and 1954, over 100 roundhouse employees were furloughed as the Company announced that all diesel repairs would be performed at the Colonie Shops, with only monthly inspections being done at Oneonta.

Master Mechanic H. M. Loucks directs removal of girders from stalls as demolition of the Oneonta Roundhouse gets underway, December, 1954. (LRHS Collection)

Although the roundhouse is now mostly gone, its spirit lives on in the memories of the men who worked there, men like Gussie Schmitt, Aaron Baker and Frank Fatta. Gussie Schmitt of Oneonta went to work in the D.& H. roundhouse in 1923 and soon became a front end and ash pan inspector, earning 25 cents an hour. In order to assume this position, he had to pass an examination administered by the Chief Engineer from Albany. Gussie soon became adept at his trade and divided his time between Oneonta and the Pennsylvania division.

Gussie's responsibilities were many, but the most important was inspection of boilers and flues. This included checking for holes and cracks in the boiler, front sheet and smoke box. Gussie also inspected the boiler for loose or broken staybolts and became so familiar with his job that he could sense a broken bolt through his wrist when it was tapped with a hammer. Gussie also oversaw the annual inspection, when the boilers were tested hydrostatically at 50% above their maximum pressure limit.

One of the most challenging tasks for boiler inspectors was the changing of flue pipes which was done once a year. This operation required two men, one at each end of the boiler. Once the beads on the flues had been broken with an air gun, the flues were driven out the front and replaced with new ones. The new tubes were installed with a 1/4" overhang on each end and a beading tool was used to seal the flues against the end sheets. Gussie considered the 1500 flues the most difficult to change as they were over 22 feet long.

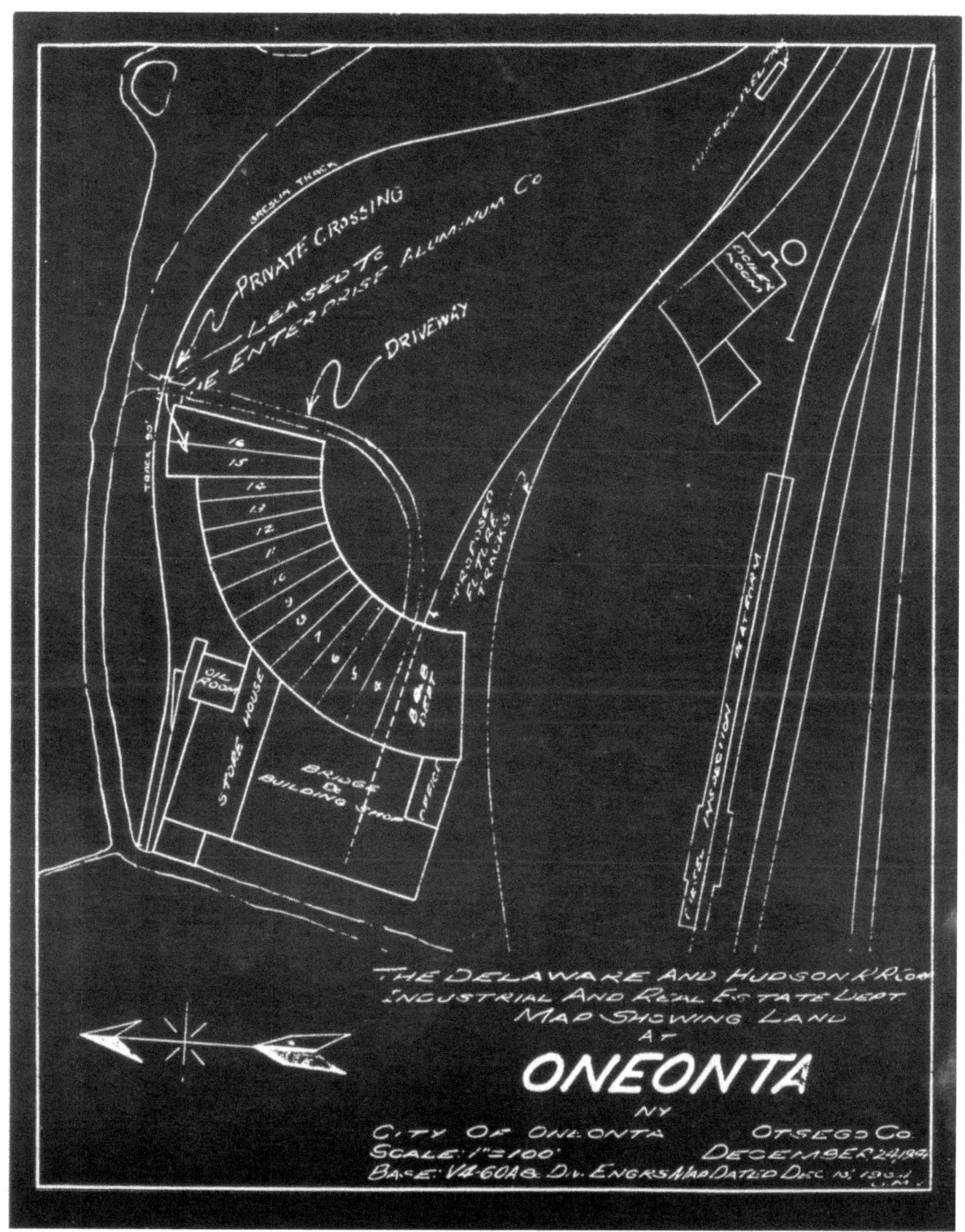

This Company blueprint shows the stall arrangement after nearly three-quarters of the Oneonta Roundhouse was dismantled in December 1954, leaving only 16 stalls intact. Three stalls were occupied by the D. & H. Bridge and Building Department, and the balance was leased to the Enterprise Aluminum Company on River Street. (LRHS Collection)

One of Gussie's most impressive skills was his ability to slide down into the boiler through the manhole in the dome cap. When asked once by a fellow worker how he managed the narrow passage, he replied that he simply tightens his belt. Once inside the boiler, pneumatic scalers were used to remove rust and corrosion and the inside surface was thoroughly checked for cracks and holes before installing the new flues.

Gussie recalls one day when tragedy struck the roundhouse complex: one of the ashpit workers was subject to seizures and apparently fell into the scalding water when no one was watching, his body not being found until the following day.

Gussie retired from the D. & H. in 1971, having spent 48 years of his life in the Oneonta Roundhouse.

Railroading was a family tradition for Aaron Baker; his father was a hostler at the D. & H. Roundhouse and in 1919 Aaron began his career with the Company as a worker in the back shop. When the facility went on strike in 1922, the roundhouse was short of manpower and Aaron seized the opportunity to transfer to a better position. His first job at the roundhouse was that of sand tender, responsible for manning the heaters that kept the sand dry so it could be dispensed to the locomotives.

After working as sand tender, Aaron transferred to the position of water tender. His new position made him responsible for checking tanks to make sure they were full and, if needed, notifying the hostler of the need to pull the locomotive out and take on water. He also had to check the fires and restart them if necessary.

Aaron eventually moved up to the position of machinist where he stayed for most of his tenure with the Company.

Aaron recalled a very interesting incident that occurred during his employ. It seems that a hostler had brought one of the locomotives out of the roundhouse and was stopped at the Master Mechanic's office to fill out a report. The hostler was apparently unaware that the engine had a leaky throttle and, before he realized what was happening, it began backing up toward the turntable gaining speed as it went. The alert cabin operator saw the engine coming and rotated the table just in time to line up the tracks with the runaway. The engine shot across the turntable, into the roundhouse and out through the back wall, finally digging into the ground near Fonda Avenue, a quarter-mile away.

Like most veterans, Aaron was not happy about the coming of the diesel age. He remembers well the early days of diesels on the line, when one of the new units stalled on Richmondville Hill and a steamer had to be dispatched to push it over the top.

Frank Fatta, a native of Davenport Center, went to work at the roundhouse in 1917 when he was 18 years old. He had to stretch his age by one year as the minimum hiring age was 19. His first job was that of boiler washer and his primary responsibility was the flushing of locomotive boilers, which was done on a monthly basis. This was accomplished by removing the plugs and pumping water at high pressure through the boiler.

After working as a boiler washer for one year, Frank bid into a position as boilermaker's helper, with the duties of cleaning up and managing tools for boilermakers. This position took him to Colonie where he spent two years before returning to Oneonta to become a boilermaker.

As a boilermaker, Frank was in charge of changing firebrick in the fireboxes each time the boilers were washed, in addition to changing flues on a yearly basis. The boilermaker had his own set of specialized equipment including caulking tools, chisels and hammers. There were also beading tools to seal the flanges on flue tubes and bobbin tools to hammer out staybolts that leaked. During his employ as boilermaker, Frank worked all three shifts. The job included both "hot" and "cold" work, depending on the temperature of the boiler. Hot work kept men warm during the winter but the disadvantage was working up a sweat and then going out into the cold air which contributed to much lost time.

After working as a boilermaker for 11 years, Frank bid into the machine shop where he stayed until his retirement in 1942 due to a back injury. He worked as a welder, spending much of his time building up and grinding flat spots on wheels in addition to repairing journal boxes. In order to continue working as a welder, it was necessary to pass a performance test every three months.

When Frank left the D. & H. in 1942, he was earning $1.10 an hour, 61 cents an hour more than he started at in 1917. This rate made him the highest paid employee in the roundhouse. Frank remembered the good days on the D. & H. when the roundhouse stalls were always full and the floors were washed every day.

The remains of the Oneonta Roundhouse, now badly deteriorated, stand as a decaying memorial to Gussie, Aaron, Frank and the hundreds of other men who gave so much of their lives to the D. & H. It is only hoped that this unique structure, like the memories of the men who served it, might somehow be preserved.

The view on the right shows the Oneonta Roundhouse remains as it appeared in summer 1992. This sight offers a stark contrast to the photo on the left, taken from the same location on March 16, 1931. (New York State Library / LRHS Collection)

EPILOGUE

The following photographs, taken by the author in the summer of 1992, are a visual survey of the remains of the Oneonta Roundhouse as it appeared at that time. Within one month, what was left of this monumental structure would be brought to the ground, leaving nothing behind but a smokestack and a pile of bricks.

This view of the outgoing track, taken between stalls 34 and 35, looks across the turntable pit to the opposite side of the roundhouse.

The remains of Oneonta Roundhouse, stalls 1 through 16, facing front of building.

Interior of Oneonta Roundhouse, looking south.

Interior of Oneonta Roundhouse, looking north.

The power plant smokestack, from stall 9, looking across the turntable pit.

Exterior of building showing the 20-foot section that was added in 1921.

Remains of the coaling tower.

Underside of coaling tower, showing two of the chutes that were used to fill tenders.

Remains of the sanding plant.

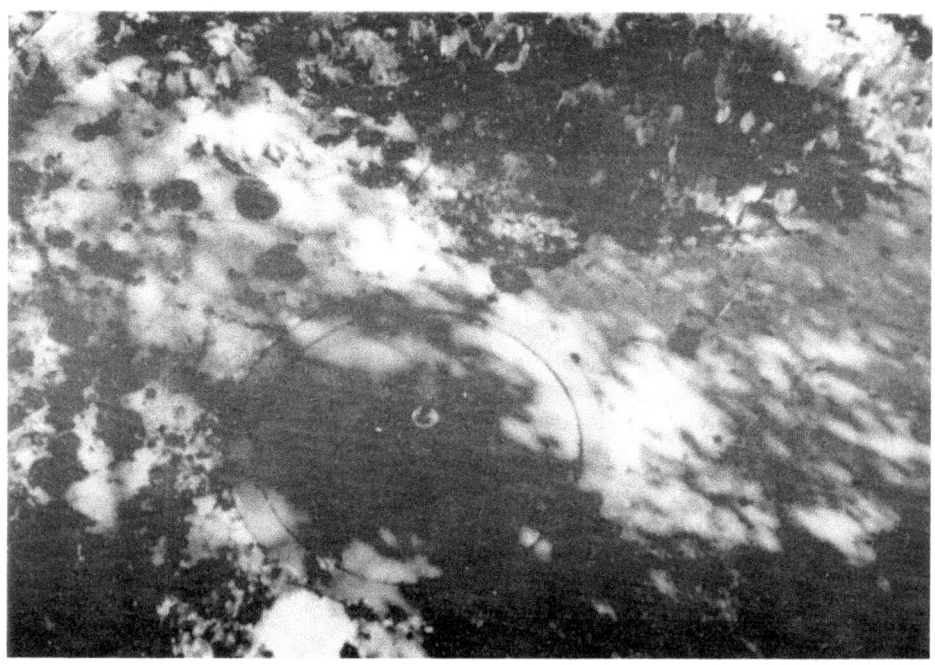

One of the 10 manholes used to access the heating conduit.

One of the 12" X 12" stone blocks which were used as rail carriers.

160 foot smokestack, installed in 1913.

Exterior of heating plant, almost completely overgrown.

Interior of heating plant with smokestack in background.

Remains of coal trestle and storage pocket.

Interior of heating plant, showing former location of boilers.

Second floor of machine shop building, showing the Master Mechanic's and the Bookkeeper's offices.

Interior of machine shop building, showing locker room and offices.

Interior of machine shop showing connecting door to roundhouse.

Interior of machine shop.

Exterior of machine shop.

Site of original machine shop, mostly overgrown.

Site of original storeroom.

Exterior of new storeroom, built in 1927.

Interior of extension added to stalls 15 and 16 in 1944 to accommodate the Challenger locomotives.

Exterior of Challenger addition.

SOURCES

American Railway Engineering and Maintenance of Way Association. *Proceedings of the Eight Annual Convention*, 1907.

Atlas of Otsego County, New York. F. W. Beers, 1868.

Baker, Harvey. "The Location of the Railroad Shops," *Oneonta Herald*, July 14, 1892.

Binghamton Press, Binghamton, December 5, 1954.

Centennial of the City of Oneonta, 1848-1948 [souvenir program]. City of Oneonta, 1948.

Delaware and Hudson Company. *A Century of Progress: A History of the Delaware and Hudson Company, 1823-1923*. Albany: J.B. Lyon, 1925.

Delaware and Hudson Company. *Annual Report of the Board of Managers*, 1921 & 1929.

Home and Abroad, Oneonta, March 12, 1870.

Insurance Map of Oneonta, Otsego County, New York. Sanborn Map Company, 1910.

Jackson, F. M. H. *Oneonta Herald* Diary, 1874-1955.

Kratville, William W. *Motive Power of the Union Pacific, Plan Package, 1869-1974*. Kratville Publications, 1978.

Moore, Edwin. *In Old Oneonta, Volume 1*. Oneonta: Upper Susquehanna Historical Society, 1962.

New Century Atlas of Otsego County, 1903.

New York State. *State Engineer's Report on Railroads*, 1871.

Oneonta 1884 Bird's Eye View, L. R. Burleigh, 1884.

Oneonta Herald, Oneonta, November 23, 1870-June 27, 1940.

Oneonta Star, Oneonta, June 9, 1905-December 20, 1954.

ALSO BY JIM LOUDON

Leatherstocking Rails is a detailed book about every railroad and trolley line that was ever built —or planned to be built—in Otsego County. Jim Loudon devotes one or more chapters to the following actual railroads: the Albany and Susquehanna; the Delaware and Hudson; the Cooperstown and Charlotte Valley; the Oneonta, Cooperstown and Richfield Springs trolley line; the Cherry Valley, Sharon and Albany; the Ulster and Delaware; and the Utica, Chenango and Susquehanna Valley, which became part of the Erie-Lackawanna. For each railroad, the author offers a chapter with a historical outline, followed by maps and photographs of each station stop and photographs of locomotives an rolling stock. He notes those station buildings still standing and those that are gone. In addition to pioneer and horse-powered railroads, he also devotes a chapter each to the Catskill, Middleburgh and Cooperstown and the Catskill Mountain and Mohawk Valley railroads that were planned but never built. The author of *The Oneonta Roundhouse*, Loudon also tells how Oneonta was the birthplace of the railroad union movement. Lavishly illustrated with over 600 photographs, maps, drawings and documents.

$39.95; ISBN-10: 0-9641119-2-6; ISBN-13: 978-0-9641119-2-9; 264 pages; 8.5" x 11", black & white interior, softcover, perfect bound, 615 illustrations.

AVAILABLE AT WWW.SQUARECIRCLEPRESS.COM

www.ingramcontent.com/pod-product-compliance
Lightning Source LLC
Chambersburg PA
CBHW080523110426
42742CB00017B/3209